M000291320

THE BETTER PART

Overcoming My Past, Answering God's Call and Living
a Fully Surrendered Life

GEORGIA HAFFENDEN

Extra MILE Innovators
Kingston, Jamaica W.I

. . . . .

Published by
Extra MILE Innovators
54 Montgomery Avenue
Kingston 10, Jamaica W. I.
www.extramileja.com

Cover Design: Promarketer, Adedolapo

Author Photo Credit: Vuong Tri Kiet
kietsphoto@telus.net

Author Contact
For consultation, feedback or speaking engagements contact the author at gh.betterpart@gmail.com

Free Resource
We have created three additional prayers to help you experience the better part God has for you. Request these prayers here and feel free to email your feedback or questions to the author at gh.betterpart@gmail.com.

To:

The men and women whom God strategically chose to mentor me as I struggled through this Christian journey.

Thank you for the biggest investment you could have ever made, that is your time to pray, encourage and counsel me as I humbled myself and answered God's call to ministry.

PRAISE FOR THE BETTER PART

"*Exposed, a preacher's journey, brokenness, sexuality, shame, rejection, condemnation, religion, church, freedom, love, purpose* are all words that represent the scope of this book. In this riveting exposé, walk with Georgia as she takes readers on a journey into the hand that life dealt...or did it? Indulge for a life-changing experience of how one woman came to know her purpose."

—Sherele Robinson
Entrepreneur

. . . . .

"You may be knocked down today but get up and begin to fight. Fight for your dreams, fight to live, fight for your destiny and let the eagle in you begin to soar" (Georgia Haffenden).

This book grabs you from the first sentence, and holds your attention page after page, as Georgia's story shows how to turn storms into unwavering victory through a relationship with God.

With deeply personal stories of her own, Georgia bares her soul with staggering vulnerability in a way that will help readers to navigate their way to freedom in Christ. In many families, there is a subtle cycle of sexual abuse that is usually swept under the carpet and more often than not, the men are protected and women and girls are made out to be perpetrators bearing the pain, hurt and stigma that sometimes continue way into adult life. As the vulnerability of my dear sister pours on these pages, may the efficacious blood of Jesus Christ erase every stain from your life, and may you be activated into your purpose for His glory and honor.

If you are ready to be vulnerable, open and honest with your past to face it head on, this book is for you. It will help to liberate you as you walk courageously in freedom. I am so proud of my sister and the victory she now walks in as she remains transparent in her quest to minister to the broken.

—Sophia Gabriel
Author, Life Coach and Minister

PREFACE

More than ten years ago, I was in a taxi returning from a class when I heard a voice speak clearly to me, saying, "You have chosen the better part." I looked around before asking my cousin who was seated next to me, "What did you say?" and she responded that she had said nothing. I thought I was going crazy because I was hearing a voice but didn't see the speaker.

On two other occasions, I heard the same voice address me with the same words; and, like the prophet Samuel, on the third occurrence I replied, "Speak, Lord, thy servant heareth." I had come to the realization that this was no ordinary voice, but rather God Himself speaking to me. I was then commanded by the Lord to read Luke 10. As I read the chapter, I was speechless as the narrative unfolded with Jesus telling Martha that Mary, her sister, had *chosen the better part*.

What was the Lord saying to me? It would take me many years to understand that this peculiar message meant that He had called me as one of His servants. As I surrendered to Him and started to walk in obedience to His will, my life became transformed.

The day I opened my heart and accepted Jesus Christ, I chose the better part, and that path continues to be a source of peace and joy, and, yes, some bittersweet moments as well. Hence, the title of this book, *The Better Part: Overcoming My Past, Answering God's Call and Living a Fully Surrendered Life.*

FOREWORD

All across the world, in every race, class and creed, women and girls continue to suffer disproportionately from gender-based violence. The World Health Organization outlines in a 2013 report, that 35 percent of women at some point in their lives experience physical violence. This is sometimes accompanied by sexual violence from an intimate partner or a non-partner.

Of concern is the fact that higher depression rates, abortions and HIV contractions are more prevalent among the women who experience these types of violence than those who do not (Global and Regional Estimates of Violence Against Women). Not only do women suffer from these forms of abuse, but sadly, many of them also lose their lives.

According to the United Nations' 2019 Global Study on Homicide, every day for the year 2017, 137 women were killed by a family member or an intimate partner. El Salvador, Jamaica, the Central African Republic and South Africa have some of the highest rates of female homicides according to this report. This trend shows strong signs of continuing, as men who grew up in homes where their fathers abused their mothers or who themselves experienced some form of violence, are more likely to be perpetrators of violence in their intimate adult relationships (Promundo and UN Women, 2017).

When one looks specifically at girls, the abuse statistics are equally worrying. UNICEF highlights for example, that 15 million girls between the ages of 15 to 19, at some point in their lives, experienced forced sexual intercourse or other sexual acts. Of this number, only one percent got professional help (UNICEF, 2017).

The Better Part takes these statistics from the global to the individual. It moves from the general to the specific and takes the reader through the harrowing, thrilling, heartbreaking yet triumphant journey of the author. The writer bares her soul as she narrates her pain, grief, uncertainties, joys and deliverance. You, too, will weep, sigh, groan, hold your breath, grieve, smile and cheer as her story becomes your story.

You see, many of us have some hurts locked in the deep recesses of our souls that we have never dared to speak about, but they are indelibly etched there. Overtime we learn to smile and nod as we mask our pain. This book confronts that façade and challenges us to take off the mask.

David in Psalm 51 v. 6 says that God desires truth in the inward parts. It is those inward parts that this book touches and brings you to a place of acknowledgement —that you, too, have suffered; not necessarily in the way or extent that the author has, but in some way, shape or form.

The Better Part tells the tale of domestic violence and abuse at the hands of caregivers and other loved ones. But it also loudly professes the salvation and deliverance found in Jesus Christ. Bit by bit, struggle by struggle, the message that there is no condemnation to those who are in Christ Jesus, reverberates across the narrative. Therefore, the message of this book is that *there is hope for even the most wretched*. Jesus, the Master Potter, is still doing His work and "there is not one broken vessel that He cannot mend."

As you come face to face with your struggles, the book reminds you that you are not alone. It brings home the point that even at our lowest, our prayers are powerful and effective (James 5:16), and that we thrive through membership in a loving and supportive community (Galatians 6:2; Hebrews 10:25).

Importantly, the author reminds us that while we may experience trauma, we have a responsibility to ourselves to seek healing. While this is a process, a great part of it includes acceptance and forgiveness. Invite the penetrating power of the Holy Spirit with you on this journey as you learn how to grieve—grieve the loss of everything that was stolen from you. Grieve the loss of every failed relationship and everything that could have been. Grieve the bad choices that you made. But, do not stay there.

Inhale and exhale and move on. Move past victimhood to victory. Move past abandonment to acceptance. Move past shame to salvation. Move past destitution to deliverance. You are God's child and Jesus died so that you can be made physically, emotionally, spiritually and mentally whole.

The Better Part shows that we can only do this with God's help, but we have a role to play. Our role is to give to God all of our lives and ask Him to heal us. Our role is to totally surrender every single part of ourselves to Him. Our role is to choose *The Better Part*.

The author is my dear friend and prayer partner. We have prayed, travailed, fasted and ministered together on numerous occasions. She is a devoted mother, intercessor, motivator, counsellor and pastor, who is very passionate about the kingdom of God. Anyone who comes in contact with her will soon realize that like Mary, she, too, has chosen *The Better Part* as she sits daily at Jesus' feet. May her story inspire you to do the same.

—Felicia A. Grey, Ph.D.
Assistant Professor of Political Science

TABLE OF CONTENTS

INTRODUCTION

Broken people tend to attract other broken people into their lives. For years, I struggled with being broken psychologically, emotionally, and sexually. I never thought that I was deserving of anything good because of how I was abused and treated. For half my life I saw myself as a 'closet child' - one who only came out of the closet whenever it was necessary. I had no friends I had anxiety about people and everything, because there was this notion in my head that people would always hurt me.

I lived in fear for a very long time and was unable to love myself or those who I considered to be family. I managed to somehow beat the odds but could not have done so until I met the most faithful man in history - Jesus Christ. Everything about my past that I thought was unjust and wicked was what He used to shape me into the woman I am today.

My brokenness led me to allow others in my life who were also broken, and in the end they, too, caused me more harm than good. I didn't have a choice in connecting with some of these persons. They were chosen for me by my parents and the others I chose. My victim mentality influenced my choices. I had no vision or dreams because I was never taught to dream, much less to have a vision by those whom God placed in my life as caregivers

Nonetheless, God, the visionary, had a master plan: one that I could not see then, but when my eyes were opened to His will, I submitted to Him in totality. As a Christian, I see my own life reflected in the biblical character, Joseph, who experienced rejection from his family and suffered as a result of their actions towards him. Nevertheless, he held on to his faith in the God of his forefathers. Thus, in the end, he fulfilled God's perfect plans for his life.

As you journey through the pages of this book, you will enter a narrative that shows how one's scars and experiences of brokenness are fertile places for God's grace to be experienced. This book will help you to experience that grace in your own brokenness, and as you walk the path of freedom. It will also help you to help others who confide in you about their scars.

Because of the freedom which I now possess in Christ, I am able to share openly about my struggles as a minister, and how that process has shaped me for the ministry in which I am presently fully engaged. As you read this book, you too will experience a profound freedom in Jesus Christ which will elevate you over your present struggles. You will also be empowered to embrace vulnerability enough to share your story of grace with others, tangibly demonstrating how you overcame and now live your better part.

CHAPTER 1
The Closet Child

It is the habit that a child forms at home, that follows them to their marriage. —Nigerian Proverb

L ife differs on many planes for each person. Some people's paths are marked by much pain and sorrow, while there are those who seem to have an easy life marked by achievement with very limited struggle. The less than desirable paths are characterized by rejection - even from in the womb, abandonment, fear and so many other negative traits. For Joseph, in Genesis 30, whose path was laden with various struggles and suffering, the trajectory of his life could have been foreseen even before he was conceived.

As it relates to my own life and the series of events that I have experienced, I see a mirror image like that of Joseph. I was born to a teenage mother and her common-law spouse who both adored me, even though the circumstances surrounding the pregnancy was not a favourable one. I can say, based on what I was told, that my father and mother loved me. However, their relationship came to an abrupt end. Years later, they both got married, a year apart, to different people. Thus, I automatically have two sets of parents comprising a stepmother and father, and stepfather and mother. I also have a stepsister and other siblings. My downward spiral began at age seven when I was taken from the comforts of my mother to go for what was supposed to be summer holidays with my father. Little did I know that the summer would morph into thirty-three traumatic years of my life! This journey saw me leaving from a place of love and security to a place of rejection, abuse, and abandonment, which opened up the door to a lifetime of struggle with low self-esteem, fear, anger, bitterness, and self-hatred. When my father took me that fateful summer, I was not brought immediately to his house, but rather to his wife's relatives who were people that I had never met before.

They were strangers and I was at a place where I knew no one. At age seven, I was at a critical stage in my physical and emotional development where I needed the comfort and protection of my mother. The intention purported by my father was for me to stay with his fiancée's relatives and get to know them until their marriage, then I would go to live with both of them.

While in the care of my stepmother's relatives, I experienced the first act of sexual molestation, and I recollect the scene as if it were yesterday. Late one evening I was called outside. I had no idea that the man in question had plans to harm me. I was not afraid to go to him because he was a member of the closely knitted family who came by every day. In my estimation, he was harmless. How naïve I was! This particular evening was not the same as evenings before. He began to speak to me in a manner that caused me to become uncomfortable. He told me, essentially, that he wanted to have a taste of me. I was flummoxed and disgusted, because here was a young man more than ten years older than me, and a professing Christian at that, telling me, a young girl, what he wanted to do to me.

Fear gripped my heart and I trembled inside, even though I had no clue what his true intentions were. Suddenly, I felt him grip my arm tightly and he pulled me to a dark place. I knew the worst was about to happen. However, I was miraculously rescued when the neighbour became suspicious and came to investigate. That night, his plan was thwarted, and I was rescued from being raped.

Another family member would come by regularly as well, and I remember how he held me down and started fondling me one day when no one was around. I fought back but he was much stronger than me. These incidents became so frequent that I felt ashamed and wanted to die. I was unable to walk and hold my head up.

Each time they came by the house I would tremble in fear and pray that I would never be alone when they came over. I felt like a target, as if I was being watched constantly, and there was no one to whom I could tell what was happening to me - no mother to run to, no father to defend me. I resorted to blaming myself and believed that something was wrong with me.

This was the first time I felt the enormous emotions associated with rejection and abandonment. The once beautiful child who was loveable, caring, and outspoken had resorted to living in a closet, and only came out when it was time for assigned chores.

Thankfully, my virginity was still intact, but I was still robbed of my innocence, and it was hard to suppress or even bounce back easily. I felt dirty and no one seemed to notice what was happening to me. I know there are many more children, women, and men with similar life experiences like mine with normal childhoods that suddenly took a turn for the worst.

Today, as you look back on the memories of your childhood, what does your heart reflect? Is it sadness, sorrow, brokenness, joy, peace or happiness? Whatever the response, God knew, even before the foundation of the earth, that some of us would have had it rough in the early stages.

The Evil Within

The time had come for me to permanently live with my father and stepmother, and to me, it was a relief. I was now able to put what had been happening to me somewhere in my subconscious and focus on being in a new home with my daddy and his wife. I breathed a sigh of relief because, finally, no more harm would come to me, and I could begin to live a normal life.

Unfortunately, that fantasy was short-lived. The truth is that my stepmother was not the nicest person, but was instead an angry and bitter woman whose wrath was about to be unleashed on me. My wounds were about to be enlarged by the venom that she spewed out when my father was not around. I experienced this and many other types of abuse in my own father's house that left me broken and shattered for years, eventually resulting in my becoming voiceless.

My father was oblivious to the things that were happening to me. The account of the storybook character, Cinderella, mirrored my life perfectly. I was not allowed to speak except when it was necessary. I was so scared of my stepmother that at either the thought or sound of her voice, I began to have serious bouts of anxiety that manifested in the form of tremors and sheer panic attacks.

As a teenager, I underwent so much that I wrestled with suicidal ideation. I thought it was better I die than continue to suffer in my father's house. I struggled with an identity crisis and didn't know who I was nor where I belonged. "Was I truly my father's child or was I adopted?" I needed answers about why was I suffering so much at the hands of those who should be loving and caring for me.

At each day's dawn my fears and anxieties came rushing back, and I found myself developing a hatred for my father whom I believed deliberately took me away from my mother. Regarding my dear, sweet mother, I resented her too, envisioning her as being wicked and uncaring to have given me away to my father to be used and abused. I hated her for not coming back for me. I convinced myself that she didn't want me in her life, and that she was perhaps happy since she too had moved on, remarried and gave birth to two more children.

It wasn't long after their marriage that my stepmother bore my father a son and there was unfettered joy and excitement in the home. This child would go on to receive the royal treatment, especially because fate ensured that he would be her sole offspring.

It was at this juncture that my stepmother brought her mom to live with us to help her care for my baby brother, and she became my rock, my saviour and guardian angel. She was a very quiet and slender elderly woman who boldly declared her feelings. While living with us she observed that her daughter's feelings toward me did not reflect how a mother should treat a daughter.

"Mama", as she was affectionately called, constantly fought for me, and for that I loved her with my whole heart. This was the first time in my life—as far as I could recall anyway—that I felt as if someone really cared for me. I believe it was her faith in Christ that caused her to show me so much love and compassion. She was a woman who loved the Lord, and each night before bed—as I shared my room with her—she would read the word of God to me, kneel with me at the bedside, and pray. Those were the times that I found solace and was able to relax, smile and be myself, knowing that someone was talking to God about me and my situation.

The Ugly in Me

Things were beginning to look up for my father as we had moved from the old house to another rented house in a quiet, residential neighbourhood. The new home would once more be tainted with memories of an unwanted human whose suffering continued. At this time, I was in my full-blown teenage years and wanted nothing to do with anyone. I lived mostly in isolation and began to exhibit behavioural problems.

I started stealing—not at home, but when I went out, especially to school. I would steal from the vendor's stalls and the supermarket. I stole little items that I honestly did not need, but I was seeking attention. I recall one day at school I stole another classmate's book, erased her name from it and wrote mine. But, unfortunately, this time I was caught, as the student realized what had happened and told the teacher, who in turn punished me and called my parents.

Can I tell you how happy I was that my dad was coming to school!

I felt no shame in what I had done; all I knew was that I would get a chance to finally see my dad and talk with him. That notion was shattered when my stepmother walked into the school by herself. When I got home, I was punished severely and was unable to go to school for a week.

When I recognized that it was not working, I stopped

stealing and resorted to hiding food as I had lost my appetite. I was a troubled teenager who was dying slowly but surely, and nothing ever turned out right for me irrespective of what I did. One day my stepmother discovered my little secret of hiding food after an unexpected overall cleaning of the house. That day she punished me so severely that I wished for death, but death would not come.

These times of suffering influenced me to pen a letter to my mother, asking why she gave me away. I asked why she didn't just have an abortion if she didn't want me in the first place. This letter wounded my mother greatly and she wept uncontrollably.

That day, I recognized that she felt as if she had failed me. It was also the day that, I believe, her hatred for my stepmother was conceived. Later, I returned to live with my mother.

The account of Joseph in the Genesis narrative shows how his brothers sold him into slavery and then lied to his father about what had happened. I, too, felt like a slave even though I was in my father's house. I felt like an ugly duckling, embracing the lies that *I was a nobody. I was unwanted and deserved whatever was meted out to me.*

Escalation of Abuse

I was still in my teenage years, and a high school student, when I became the caregiver to my brother and father. My stepmom had relocated to another country and I returned to my dad's home to help care for my little brother. I was now the one with the responsibility of taking care of the house, ensuring that they had clean clothes and food to eat daily. While being a caregiver for my brother, my male cousins began to devour my flesh. I became the sex object they used to fulfil their sexual appetite. I had no choice as my father had to work the graveyard shifts and he would leave us with an aunt who lived close by. My father was happy to have this support and felt at peace while at work, believing that we were safe with his sister. But it was just the opposite.

Daily, they would individually sexually molest me. It became so bad with one in particular because he was aggressive toward me, and instilled a strong sense of fear that, whenever I saw him, I trembled. Once again, I longed for death, but it still would not come. I longed to be rescued but it never materialized. I began to experience excessive anxiety around my family. I would tremble until I could hear my teeth rattling in my head. I wept uncontrollably and begged my father not to leave me at that aunt's house, but my cries went unheard.

My greatest fear was that one day one of my cousins would end up savagely raping me. Once when my cousin attempted to have his way with me, my aunt's husband flicked on the lights to check on us and he saw the unimaginable. He immediately called my aunt who came running to see what had transpired. He told her what he saw, and my aunt ran up to me and slapped me across the face, accusing me of wanting to sleep with her son. Yes! She accused me of wanting to sleep with her son.

Thankfully his intentions were shattered but I was left traumatized. The skeleton was now out of the closet and I was no longer just a broken vessel, but a shattered one as well. Her reaction made me fear what my father was going to do with me. That evening I cried out to God like I never had in my life, and I believed He heard me.

When my dad came home, he was told their version of the story. As I prepared for the worst, he gently called me and said, "Talk to me. Tell me what happened." For the first time my father wanted to hear my side, and I had no choice but to tell him the truth about what was taking place with me.

God showed me that He was with me and that He heard my plea. My father came to my rescue. He believed me, stood up for me and defended me. My paternal family then labelled me the "black sheep" of the family. That was the day my heart hardened against my paternal family and I resented them.

I was a victim of circumstances and situations that I had no control over. These events had shaped me to believe that I was worth nothing. Love and family had left a bitter taste in my mouth. I eventually left my father in search of a place of peace and comfort and went to my mother. But it appeared that even there, the demon of sexual abuse found me and tried to further subject me to a vicious cycle of sexual abuse.

Strength for the Broken

In reading this chapter, you may be feeling overwhelmed right now because you can possibly relate to this story. If this is the case, I pray right now that you will not repress what you are feeling but let it all go.

Holy Spirit, here is someone whose journey from childhood to adolescence has been marked by many scars that have left them with the residue of bitterness, fear, or possibly hatred. I thank You Lord that, even then, You had a plan that they would no longer be a slave to their fear. Help them to let go of all the pain and hurt that their families and others have caused them to bear. Thank You, Lord, that You are working on perfecting all that concerns them. Amen.

If you have not experienced anything like sexual abuse, but know the pain of being emotionally and/or verbally abused, may the Holy Spirit strengthen you to face who you were then and guide you to where you want to be, as you strive for emotional wellness and a deeper walk with Christ.

Some of our deepest scars come, not from people who are strangers, but from those who we know and trust implicitly. Sometimes it is our families that break us in unimaginable ways. Believers in Christ need a community which will give us a sense of belonging, which will embrace us and help us walk through these gray areas that need repair.

CHAPTER 2
Knocked Down by the Unexpected

"Reality is not neat, not obvious, not what you expect."
—C.S. Lewis

My adult years were no different from my childhood and teenage years. Nothing much had changed – I was nothing, just a human being existing in a physical body. I was fighting an internal battle which was more than I could handle.

Persons saw me as this outspoken and brilliant young woman, but I could not accept it, and neither could I accept a mere compliment such as "You are beautiful." Life for me sucked and I was tired of living it. After graduating from High School, I wanted to return to further my education, but my father was financially incapable of funding it, so I began to apply for jobs.

I also decided to go back to evening classes and garner a few more subjects, and this was where an unexpected miracle happened to me. In the process of re-sitting Mathematics, the Vice Principal from my alma mater approached me. She was

15

the invigilator for the exam and said she wanted to see me right after the exam ended. When we met, she only requested that I go home, do a résumé and take it to her the following day. I was speechless but did as I was told.

The next day I attired myself professionally and went to see the Vice Principal. I don't know what I was thinking, but that morning I followed my gut instinct to dress professionally.

She handed me a pile of résumés and told me to go to the hospital and give them to the Chief Executive Officer. When I was called into the CEO's office, she interviewed me on the spot, and I was officially hired for my first ever job in a governmental institution. This was some achievement as the CEO was very impressed with my interview. She mentioned that she was going to hold me to my word that I would work and go back to school to get a career. I was over the moon! This was the first time ever that something good had happened to me and I had someone looking out for me to succeed.

When the Unexpected Happened

I was only a few months into my job when I discovered that I was pregnant. Two months prior, a close cousin of mine had introduced me to her boyfriend's cousin and we became friends. I was nineteen, he was twenty-three, and he wasted no time in telling me that he wanted a relationship. I didn't know what dating or courting was and we didn't really do any of that. I never knew what true love meant but I was mesmerized by the full attention that he was giving me.

My parents never taught me my worth and I never heard the words: "I love you," "You are special," or "You can do whatever you set your mind to." My boyfriend knew nothing about my past and didn't take the time to know me well. I didn't share anything with him either. I felt that whatever little he knew about me was good enough for him, fearing that if he knew about my horrible past he would certainly leave.

My dad became aware that I was seeing someone as I began to come home later and later. He tried to warn me about my change in behaviour, but it was too late to try and correct me. One thing he said stood out to me though, "Whatever you are looking for out there, you will find it." His statement made me angry and told him that if he was speaking about pregnancy it wouldn't happen to me.

Within a few weeks of hearing my father speak those words, I was pregnant. Shortly after, my relationship began to deteriorate, and I had no choice but to tell my dad about this development. He reacted very differently from the way I expected, and only wanted to know if my boyfriend would stand up to his responsibility. Besides, he indicated, I was late in finding out because he had already seen the changes in my body signaling that I was pregnant.

Four months into the pregnancy my boyfriend and I started having a series of arguments. It eventually seemed as though we had become enemies. I had told him that I needed time to be by myself, that I wanted us take a break from seeing each other, but he would not have that. One evening, he came to visit me after his shift ended and an argument developed.

He had brought some things for me and I became furious because I told him I needed a break. In anger, I threw the bag down and he, in turn, became upset and slapped me across the face. That was the day I officially ended the relationship because I did not want to end up like my stepmother's sister who had lost her life due to domestic violence.

When my dad heard that my boyfriend hit me he went to defend me. Afterwards, my boyfriend still came around as he thought that I was not serious; but as time passed, he realized that I was not backing down from what I had said. Eventually he got the message and we separated. I was nineteen, pregnant and living with my father.

Words are important. From God speaking things into being in Genesis we see the power of the spoken word throughout the Bible. As a parent today, I have learned that when children are deprived of words of affirmation, they are likely to struggle with low self-esteem, depression, and even their sexuality. Later, they tend to gravitate to the first person who appears to be meeting that long- awaited need for love and affection.

I already saw myself as a failure and life had now knocked me down again. What was I going to do? How was I going to manage as a parent? The only thing that kept me going was the fact that I was working my own money. My father cared for me too, and he, along with my mother, became my biggest supporter.

When Shame Becomes My Garment

The news of my pregnancy was spreading like wildfire everywhere, and what was most humiliating is that I had only been working at my job for less than a year. My Supervisor called me into her office one day, and told me that the CEO requested to see me. To my surprise, the CEO started the meeting by asking for my father who happened to be her friend. I told her that he was on vacation overseas.

Her response was, "No wonder I am not getting through to his phone." I didn't know why she was so adamant about speaking with my dad, but she would later tell me why.

She proceeded to call our family doctor into the meeting, looked directly into my eyes and said, "It has been brought to my attention that you are pregnant. Is this factual?"

With my head held down in shame I responded, "Yes." She proceeded to ask if my father knew, how far along I was, and who was the man responsible. I opened up and revealed that I was in my sixth month. She was dumbfounded because I carried a small tummy.

After listening to me, she began to speak to me like a mother who was disappointed in her daughter. She angrily inquired about my dreams of going back to school and getting a career. "Where is the young lady I interviewed a few months ago?" she lamented.

She saw the shame on my face and the pain in my eyes and changed her tone to a softer one and said, "When I interviewed you, you told me of your desire to go back to school, so what happened?" I had nothing to say because I was not used to this amount of attention. The CEO of this organization was telling me how disappointed she was in me and asking if I was going to let my dreams die. Instead of feeling more shame, I felt a glimmer of hope that someone had cared enough for me to see that I had fallen off track by getting pregnant and needed some tough love.

I had a child growing inside me, one that I was not prepared for, and I had serious anxieties about what kind of mother I would be because I was not ready to be a parent. Nonetheless, I was determined to move forward, although before long I was the subject of gossip on my job. I felt lonely, and based on what the CEO had said I didn't know if I would have a job after my delivery.

Could my life get any worse than this? It did!

This time I was hit so hard that only God's grace brought me back. In my seventh month of pregnancy, one evening I was on my way out, and while walking to the bus stop a car stopped at my feet. It was a close family friend. We talked and he inquired where I was going and offered to take me. He called my dad "Uncle' and each of my aunts 'Auntie,' so I had no reason to fear being alone with him.

He drove up to a house close to where I lived, which he occupied with two of my cousins, and invited me in. He said, "Just come inside and sit while I freshen up, then we will be on our way." I didn't hesitate to go in and he proceeded to give me a tour of the house. However, when he reached the bedroom, he started doing things that made me very uncomfortable.

I was not having that one bit. I fought him off but he forcibly pushed me on the bed. I was heavily pregnant. I was crying and begging him, "Please don't do this. I am pregnant." But it was all in vain. He raped me without any thought of the unborn child in my womb. I was devastated! I didn't even know if he had worn any form of protection. All I knew was that I wanted the earth to open up and swallow me, and I went home to wallow in my sorrows.

CHAPTER 3
New Life, Inner Turmoil

"We're going to have to let truth scream louder to our souls
than the lies that have infected us."
—Beth Moore

Two months later, I gave birth to a beautiful baby girl via Caesarean section who I was unable to love. I felt as if I had failed to protect her; plus I was already a messed-up woman who had so much going on internally.

Daily, I would hold this child while breastfeeding her and crying uncontrollably. I didn't realize that I was suffering from postpartum depression which went untreated for a long time. My mother was there for me as she knew this was my first child. Every day she came from her home to assist me. My best friend at the time was also there. I felt their presence and support, but I was only present bodily—my mind was elsewhere.

Moreover, I was so tired of living that I contemplated taking my life. Yes! This time, I had it all planned out and was about to execute my plan. I had taken two bottles of my father's prescription medication from his room and laid them out on the washroom floor. I sat there with them for at least an hour, sobbing bitterly.

I didn't see any reason to live anymore, so I opened the bottles, and just as I was about to take them, I heard a voice loudly say, "Before you do, go and call your friend." I resisted and moved again to take the pills, but that voice wouldn't leave me alone, so I went and made the call. I told my friend to ensure she took great care of my daughter and that I loved them. I told her to tell my family that I am tired and couldn't live anymore.

She begged me to give her 10 minutes to come and see me and, faithful to her word, she quickly left her job (we worked at the same organization) and arrived in that timespan. She grabbed me in a massive embrace and wept with me on the floor, encouraging me that we were going to do life together.

I believe God intervened that day by speaking to me and compelling me to make that call. My friend and I became inseparable, and today she is my daughter's godmother.

After this, I continued on without seeking help for my postpartum depression, but at least my friend was there consistently. I was a single mother and very withdrawn. I would go out now and then but was dead on the inside. I still lived with my dad and brother, but there was nothing much to talk about.

Sometime later, my mom decided to take my daughter to live with her and I ended up going there as well, but things were very shaky with us. I was not adjusting well to my mother's side of the family because I felt like an outcast, and my stepfather and I had no relationship at all. I thought that maybe things would have been a little different, but once more I felt the brutal hands of men who wanted to have their way with me.

A Life-Changing Encounter

One day while at work, a man rushed in with his relative who had tried to commit suicide. I helped him and his family to the best of my ability, and before he left the hospital that night, he came to say 'Thank you', and we exchanged numbers. I had been walking around with his number for several weeks in my pocketbook, and then one day as I started to empty out my pocket book I threw away the number.

Unexpectedly, I received a call from him one evening and we began to talk constantly until it matriculated into a relationship. There was something different about this man, separate from the fact that he was twenty-five years older than me. He was tender, treated me with respect and honestly cared about me. He devoted his entire being to me by taking the time to get to know me.

We spent so much time together that I grew to love him deeply, and we couldn't get enough of each other. Later on, as the relationship grew, he disclosed that he was married but his wife was in the United States, and he had returned home because of unforeseen circumstances. I was only a little bothered by the disclosure. My thoughts were that he was here and she was there, and my attitude literally was, "who cares?"

This man had a way of connecting with me on every level, and I never thought for a second that he was God-sent to change my life in a way that I would never imagine. I introduced him to my parents and family, and he knew the details about most of what I had been through in my life. One evening as we laid in bed, he began to talk to me about God, and how he was brought up in the church, but had strayed.

I was very still and said nothing. He realized that he had gotten my attention, and proceeded to tell me more and more about Jesus. It eventually became a pattern that each time he would come around he would talk to me about Jesus; and one day in particular, he took his Bible with him on one of our dates in the park. I began feeling confused and asked him if he was crazy. How could he be having sex with me and telling me about Jesus?

"What's up with that and who in the hell does that?" He told me he was a backslider but there was something about me that was propelling him to tell me about Jesus. As we met weekly, he read the Bible to me, prayed with me, and sent me home to read and ponder what I had heard. I couldn't comprehend what was happening. How could I process this? All I knew was that this was having an imperceptible impact on me, but I didn't say much either way.

Over time, I became concerned about the relationship and I wanted more. I was consumed by my own feelings since this man was unlike any I had encountered, and I wanted him to always be in my life. He was both tender and respectful towards me.

I had not yet recognized that God had sent this man to deposit into me exactly what I needed: *The Word of God*. One night, he and I were having a phone conversation, and something in me just snapped. I became angry and upset because I needed to know where I stood in this relationship. Was he ever going to sort out his divorce? I ended the conversation abruptly by hanging up the phone on him and went into a tantrum. My thoughts were all over the place, but I guess it was a good place to be because something extraordinary happened to me that night.

I was sobbing, crazy over a married man, and I wanted him to do whatever he had to do so we could be together. As I continued crying, suddenly I felt the presence of someone or something in the room. My face was turned to the wall, so I called out, "Daddy. Daddy, is that you?" But no one answered.

I laid there for a few more minutes, then I heard my name called once more. I answered and went to see if my dad was calling me. Of course, he said he wasn't. I went back to bed and the voice called me two more times, and then I answered, "Yes, Lord."

Next came a question, "Are you happy?"

I answered, "No. How can I be happy when I don't have You?"

At first, I thought that I was going crazy and didn't say anything about it. I told the guy I was dating the next day about this experience, and he pointed me to the narrative of 1 Samuel 3 when God called Samuel.

Armed with my report on this experience, he became more persistent in feeding me the Word, and he kept on saying that he believed strongly that God had a plan for my life, and that He is going to use me to speak into the lives of people.

One afternoon he declared: "One day, the student shall surpass the teacher." During this time, he was not only giving me the Word of God, but he was helping me to develop confidence in myself. He spoke to my soul by using the Word of God to get me to start seeing and thinking about myself differently.

He told me that God had a plan for my life and that I had not seen anything yet. "Me! Oh please! Can God even use someone like me? Look at all that I have been through and was still going through. That's not possible!"

I believe he saw something in me that I could not see, and he kept me centered in the Word of God, while attempting to pull out purpose from within me. It was not long after this that I went to work one day on frontline duty, when this familiar voice appeared once more, asking me three times whether I was happy. This time the 'voice' went on further to state "It is now or never".

I ran from the front desk into my Supervisor's office crying, and indicating to the persons inside that the Lord was calling me and what His message was.

That morning a staff member came into the office whose father was a pastor. She called him and asked if he could speak with me. I took the phone and told him what had happened, and he asked me what I wanted to do. On that day, I accepted Jesus right there in that office, and set the date for water baptism two weeks later.

When the weekend for my baptism came, I told my father that I was going to spend the weekend with my co-worker and go to church with her. I was going to be baptized that Sunday but felt afraid to tell anyone because I felt they would have asked me if I was serious and really ready.

Sunday came, and out of all the other new converts at the church, I was the only one who took my water baptism on a beautiful white beach in my home country, Jamaica, with my pastor, his daughter, and an evangelist from the church. I was the happiest woman! I felt an unspeakable joy bubbling deep within me. That morning when I went to church, I couldn't even stand to give my testimony because I was so overwhelmed that I was now a child of God.

Hope for the Broken

I don't know what you have been through in your life but if you have at any time experienced feelings of inferiority, worthlessness, shame, guilt, suicidal ideation or even attempted suicide, there is nothing to be ashamed of. Do not beat up on yourself! Life has a way of bringing challenges that may knock us down, but we are meant to rise up.

You may be knocked down today but get up and begin to fight. Fight for your dreams, fight to live, fight for your destiny and let the eagle in you begin to soar. Everything that has happened in your life thus far has formed character in you. You, Dear Reader, are built to last; therefore, amidst all that has happened in your past, you are destined to reign.

CHAPTER 4
Answering God's Call

"For many are called, but few are chosen."
—Matt. 22:14 (NLT)

There was so much that I didn't understand about God, but I was eager to learn. Family and friends now knew that I had taken this bold step. Some were happy while others were already passing their verdict as to how long I was going to remain a Christian. This did not deter me. I knew that I had made the best decision to enter into a covenant relationship with Jesus Christ. I had told my significant other that I had now become a born-again Christian and he was very happy for me.

He continued to encourage me to study the Word of God and ensured that I spent quality time with the Lord. He, too, recommitted his life to the Lord and went back to church, though his was separate from mine. He was very supportive, while my mother was extremely happy that I was now a child of God. I went to church consistently, making a lot of sacrifices, because it was not close to my home. Oftentimes I would pack a weekend bag and go to my pastor's house for the weekend so I could go to church on Sundays, because I wanted to honour my relationship with God.

Months turned into years and I found myself in a particular season doubting my spiritual life. Even though I was a Christian and walking with the Lord, my issues were still there, and I continued to battle with my past. I became a prisoner of my past, and kept losing the battle because when it became unbearable, I reached out to none other than the older man whom I had been in a relationship with. It was he who understood me more than anyone else, and I believed he could help me deal with my emotional state of mind.

Bowing to My Flesh

I was naïve to the fact that I was setting up myself to become a slave to sexual sins, and to also cause this man – who had recommitted his life – to fall into my web. One evening we cried together and asked God for His forgiveness. The next thing I knew he asked me to marry him and I said "Yes." I was now an engaged woman and that was what I believed would wipe away the shame of fornication, but that was short-lived.

My mother sat me down one day and asked me if I was sure this is what I wanted, and what was the status of his divorce. I was adamant that I needed this, and preparations were being made for our private wedding in another parish. After my mom finished speaking with me, I left the house for a long walk.

I then fell to the ground on the sidewalk of a lonely street and cried out to God, asking Him to let His perfect will be done in my life. I told God if this was not the man for me to just let me know. No one understood what I was going through: he was the only person that cared for me and, in my head, they just wanted to mess things up for me.

As a young Christian, I had no one to guide me. Most of what I saw in the church amounted to condemnation and judgement – even if you simply sat beside a male outside of the church, you were judged. We were trying to make the sex holy by getting married.

The wedding was not going to be the talk of the town because it was small and intimate with only four persons. The pastor who was scheduled to do the wedding, for some reason, couldn't be reached via the phone for at least a week; and when I finally got through to him, he gave me a fixed date for the wedding.

My mother reluctantly gave me her blessings and off I went to St. Thomas where the wedding would take place; but before I did, I stopped to see my soon-to-be-husband. For some reason when I saw him that afternoon, something was off with him. He didn't seem happy. I asked him what was happening, but he reassured me that all was well. He told me I should go ahead of him since he would join me the next day. He gave me his suit and I went on my way feeling very happy that I was going to be married to the man I loved – a man who also loved me.

We had been in a relationship for four years, and after I became a Christian we had stopped talking intimately and separated for a good six months. When I got to St. Thomas, arrangements were already in motion. I had bought a simple outfit, but there was a beautiful wedding gown waiting for me, and cakes as well. My host informed me of the plans for the wedding that Saturday. I was uneasy, but went ahead with the preparations.

The pastor called me the night before the wedding and started to inquire about the groom. He asked the necessary questions for the paperwork, and when he inquired about his status, whether he was a bachelor, I didn't know what that meant. When he explained what the word meant, I told him he would have to speak with my partner. That night I was unable to sleep; I was restless and felt in my heart that things were simply falling apart.

Early the next morning, I woke up with little tingles of excitement because it was my wedding day. I had taken up the suit my fiancé gave me and started ironing it when the house phone rang. I overheard my host, who was the connection to the pastor, trying to answer some questions, but she seemed to be struggling. Based on the answers – or lack thereof – I overheard her giving, I felt my heart beginning to sink, and knew instinctively that I would not be getting married that day.

In my moment of distress, I heard that now familiar voice say, "There will be no wedding." I was broken-hearted and the tears began to flow. God had to show up and intervene at the worst possible time!

He wanted me to know that He had plans for me, but I was not at a place to listen to Him. I needed my fleshly desires sorted out, and what better way to do so than get married, even if it was not part of God's plan and purpose for me.

My host later passed the phone to me, and the pastor who was actually on the line said that he could not conduct the wedding based on what was disclosed to him by my so-called fiancé who, by the way, was still married. My world was shattered...I felt like a fool.

I was in shock, but apart from that I felt that God's hands were all over this. That weekend should have been one of celebration, but there was so much sorrow, leading to a sequence of tragic events which kept occurring. I took them as signs that I was not to get married to this man.

Even though we loved each other so much, it just was not meant to be. He eventually came to see me later that evening. That was the day I told him that it was over, and that I never wanted to have anything to do with him again.

God's Agenda

Afterwards, we went our separate ways. I went home in my shame and disgrace, not knowing how to face my mother. I brought home the cake and told her what unfolded, and she began to praise the Lord, insisting that God answered prayers. I wanted what I thought was best for me because I was a broken young woman. He was the first man who never abused me or treated me like a nobody. He had earned the respect of my family, and because of that I wanted the security and legal right to have sex without feeling guilty for it.

Looking back, God indeed had a plan for me, but at that time I couldn't see it. I believed that this man came into my life at a time when I needed a Saviour. The plan was not for a relationship, but for him to impart the Word of God to me so that it could take root in me, and bring me to a place to receive God's salvation. The events that unfolded were due to my vulnerability and my faulty thinking that any man who came my way only wanted my body.

Each person who comes into our lives is not meant to be in an intimate relationship with us. I understand that clearly now. It took a while for me to recover from the cancellation of the wedding, but it brought me to a place that I needed to be, and that was in the presence of God.

I became intentional about walking the path of righteousness and wanted Jesus' will, above all else, to be done in my life. I believe that it takes something drastic at times for us to walk the path that God has set for us. This was my turnaround season, and it was at this point in time that my desire for the Lord became like no other.

I realized I needed to do something, and that God's hand was upon my life. I needed to be free, I needed more of God. Even though I was no longer going to my home church, I strongly needed to know more, so I started to visit other churches and observe the different modes of worship. A friend who knew that I was at a crossroads in my life invited me to a fasting service.

I considered it for a while, and then once when it was my day off from work, I went. It began at 10 a.m. and ended at 6 p.m. It was such a blessing that I became hooked. The environment kept me pressing and pushing for the will of God to be done in my life. Men and women prayed earnestly and feasted on the Word of God. At the end, people's needs were prayed for.

I never missed a week, and each time I went back I hungered for the things that were being taught, and the manifestation of the power of God was rich in that place. I began to develop a hunger and thirst after God that I could not contain. Wherever the leader of the fasting was invited to minister, I would go. This newness I was experiencing also compelled me to begin to surround myself with people who were of like passion.

This newfound love and desire propelled me into hot pursuit of God. I began to zealously and diligently study His Word, as well as spending days and nights in constant prayer. I bought all the books I could get on Christianity as I was desirous of knowing all I could about Jesus.

I would shut up in my room days upon days – fasting, praying, and studying the Word of God. I continued to go to the fasting services and, as I continued, I began to experience growth in my walk with the Lord, and the people kept me desirous of pressing forward.

What I was experiencing opened my eyes to what I believed King David experienced when he penned Psalm 42:1-2, "As the deer pants for the water brooks, so pants my soul for You,

O God. My soul thirsts for God, for the living God. When shall I come and appear before God?" (NKJV). I was thirsty for God and became so consumed with spending time with Him that I no longer cared much for anything.

My priorities were different, and I wanted to experience Him in any way I could. On one occasion, I went away to a friend's house and shut myself away doing three days of absolute fasting. I wanted to hear from God, I desired to know what His plans were for me. I needed to get His attention and fasting was my way of doing so.

I was twenty-five years old at the time when I did that fast, and it was that fast that broke the shackles and chains off my life. I recalled that on the second day of the fast, I was led to write down my age and all those who had hurt me and caused me much sorrow and pain. Afterwards, I cried out to God, asking Him to heal me from the time I had experienced the first hurt until the age of twenty-five.

I also inquired of the Lord about why my stepmother treated me the way she did, and He revealed it to me and commanded me not to make it known until it was time. I learned through this process that we hold on sometimes to some people because they meet a need or longing in us that was never met in our lifespan.

On the other hand, we fail to see that some people were brought into our lives to get us to a point that would create a change in us.

Oftentimes, if we refuse to let go and continue to pursue the relationship, we wound our own selves because they had done their time. Do not allow your past choices and circumstances to determine how you move forward in life. Be open to the fact that God has a plan for your life, and it involves all the pain and hurt that you have experienced. God may be calling you right now to walk in His perfect plan for your life, and in so doing you are about to walk into a purpose that is greater than when you answered the Lord Jesus initially. I have come to understand that we can allow brokenness to be the weapon that forms our decisions, and in the end, we allow ourselves to become prisoners to our own imposed wills.

Prayer for the Broken

Holy Spirit, I ask you to help your son or daughter right now to be sensitive to your voice, as You call them to a place where Your will can be established in their lives. Holy Spirit, may you help those who are struggling with their flesh to be still and know that you are God, as You help them to persevere in waiting on You.

CHAPTER 5
The Battle for Purpose

"A big part of being a well-adjusted person is accepting that
you can't be good at everything."
—Kelly Williams Brown

Finally, there were so many good things happening in my life that I believed that there was more to me than I had thought. Many persons witnessed the transformation which was taking place in my life, and some began to ask questions about my experience. I had become more open and found myself in the company of a few women of faith who took me under their wings. One was an elderly woman who was the leader of the fasting service I spoke about in the previous chapter.

What was most fascinating about her was that she was from the Christian Brethren denomination which historically didn't allow women to have any form of a leadership role in local assemblies. Her husband was an elder at the church and both of them worked together in this ministry, but she would not allow their rules to deter her from fulfilling God's purpose. She requested the use of the church every Wednesday to host the fasting service.

Her devotion to her calling and how she mentored us stirred a great desire in me to want to become a vessel used by God. I faithfully went to the weekly fasting service, ensuring that the shift I worked didn't cause me to miss even one meeting. There I became exposed to what ministry was like, learning from the various ministers who came from other churches within the community to lead and participate. My faith in God began to take on new levels, and I hungered for what I saw. I didn't know what God was up to, but all I knew was that these men and women saw something in me, a purpose that was so great that they invested in me spiritually.

It was a new season in my life, and I was basking in the glory of it. In this season, I sensed that God was moulding me for greater things that I could not yet comprehend, and I didn't want to miss out on those. I recall that the fasting group was invited to its sister church's women's weekend retreat in Kingston, Jamaica. I was excited about this and ensured I would be there. When the time came, I went to the retreat with an open heart and mind, but with a great expectation that I wanted to experience God in a different way.

It was at this retreat that I met other women of God whose testimonies greatly impacted me, and their stories gave me renewed hope in Jesus Christ, proving that no matter what we are facing God certainly shall perfect that which concerns us. There was one lady in particular at the retreat with whom I found favour, and she took me under her wings at the retreat. I kept in contact with her afterwards and was invited over to her house to spend the weekend. I admired how she was so gentle towards her husband, and the manner in which they spoke to each other amazed me. I wasn't used to seeing that in a relationship, and I thank God for allowing me to experience this. I thought to myself that they were certainly putting into practice what the Scriptures said about honouring each other

That evening they prayed over me during devotion. Things started to look better for me, and this elderly woman encouraged me to begin to dream, and to write down the visions of the things I wanted to see happen in my life.

God often uses people to help to shape our character, and what I experienced at that house that weekend showed me that a man and his wife can live in peace and harmony, no matter the struggles they face. Step by step, God was creating avenues for me to grow, and he used these people to deposit in me the different things that would help me along my journey.

The Birthing of Purpose

Like John Wesley who knelt daily by his bedside for hours crying out to God for spiritual renewal, I, too, took the principle I read in Tommy Tenney's book, *The God Chasers*, and began to cry out for my revival/spiritual renewal. I believe that God heard my plea and began to answer my prayers. Strange things began to happen to me, and I couldn't comprehend it.

I began to have dreams and visions that would come to pass. Whenever I prayed for persons, I would find myself speaking things to them that had to do with their past, present or future. Some dreams I didn't speak about, but would watch them come to pass as time progressed.

It was then that I realized that God was truly an instrumental force in my life, and over time I began to trust His leading. As the opportunities to minister became more frequent, things would happen in relation to the gift of prophecy, and I, too, began to experience this gift at work in my own life.

On a consistent basis, while ministering, I would hear that familiar voice which I came to recognize as the voice of the Holy Spirit, speak to me during times of ministry. He would tell me to do things and speak things that caused persons to be in awe of the wondrous power of God.

I recall one particular time I went to a revival, and while I was ministering the Holy Spirit impressed on my heart to speak prophetically to a man concerning his wife, that they would have twin children – a boy and a girl. A year later they welcomed their twins – a boy and a girl – just as the Lord had spoken through me. I also discovered that I had developed a passion and love for preaching and teaching the Word of God.

My story was changing. I was no longer that feeble young woman who had no vision or dreams. I invited God into my story and He completely began to rewrite the script. I became pregnant with God's purpose when I began to spend quality time in His presence by diligently studying His Word and spending a lot of time in prayer.

I recall there was a time when I was so hungry for God that, every evening after my shift ended, I would be in a hurry to go home because I had an appointment to keep and that was to be with God. I would shut up in my room reading the word of God and spend hours in prayer. Whatever I read I would pray back to God. I believe that during those times God was building me and preparing me for the work that He had called me to do.

I had humbled myself and surrendered completely to the Lord, seeking His will for my life, and in so doing God began to exalt me. I was now in the company of Pastors, Evangelists, Preachers and Teachers of the Word of God. I was honored to be a part of this group of leaders, and before I knew it, I began to travel not only locally but internationally as well.

During those times of ministry, I remember the numerous prayers that were sent up for me, and the prophetic words that came forth concerning what God was going to do in my life, and how He would use me.

Not only had things changed for me spiritually, but God supernaturally opened the door for me to go back to school. This was something that I had prayed about for six years.

I use the term *supernaturally* because I was in the process of applying to numerous educational institutions in Jamaica and abroad. However, one morning I was at work and was called to the emergency room to register a client. On my way to do so, I greeted the doctor on duty, and he asked how I was. I said, "Sir, I am blessed and highly favoured by God." His immediate response to me was, "Georgia, go register the client and then come see me in my office."

I had no idea that this insightful doctor was also a pastor. He spoke into my life that day and prayed for me saying, "It's time for you to go back to school, and this time you are to attend a Bible College." I was in awe!

"Me? Bible school?" I queried. He told me that I should give him a day or two and he would get back to me. Honouring his word, two days after he called and told me that I should call the Jamaica Theological Seminary, find out what the qualifications were, and then apply once I met the criteria.

My pastor's niece who was assisting me in the process of applying to schools called me that very day. She told me to apply to a particular school in Kingston. It was the same Seminary that the doctor told me to call. I recognized then that God was ordering my steps, and little by little He was fulfilling His purpose in my life.

Finally, in 2006, my dream of enrolling in higher education materialized, and I entered the Jamaica Theological Seminary to pursue a degree in Social Work. I was excited about this new season of my life.

God had also opened the door for me financially to study without having the stress of paying tuition. When I was about to resign from my job, I had gone to another doctor to do my physical for school, and she asked what field I was going to study and when I would be leaving. I gave her the information she asked for.

She further asked if I would return to work in the summer and I told her that I was resigning. She would have none of that and called the Head Office to speak to someone. She told me to report to the office the next Monday morning at 9:00 a.m. for an interview.

I was successful and offered four years of study leave with pay, and had half of my tuition paid for the four years. I didn't even know who a Social Worker was, but one thing I knew for sure was that when I inquired at the school about the programs offered, the Dean of Admissions told me to be prayerful about my program choice, and I took her advice.

With the leading of the Holy Spirit I chose the Bachelor of Social Work. My father brought me on the main campus on Saturday, January 15, 2006, and on January 16, 2006 the Sunday morning following, while getting dressed to go to the Dedication Service for new students, I fell down a flight of stairs, breaking my left foot in two places.

What an amazing way to start the semester! I was immediately rushed to the hospital. Thankfully, I didn't have to go back home as the School Administration allowed me to attend classes on crutches.

Even though I had a rough start at the Seminary, I became part of a very supportive community. Different persons made themselves available to assist me with getting my assignments done, and today, one in particular has become my bosom friend. It was at the Seminary I discovered that I truly had potential, and worked hard to achieve the degree.

There were moments I wanted to give up because there were so many challenges, but my bosom buddy – who turned out to be a youth pastor from the church group in which I was baptized – became a constant support to my success.

Deception and Yielding to Temptation

God did not only rewrite my story, but He had also given me a platform, and I was using it to enhance His kingdom. I was now a woman on a mission: preaching and teaching the Word of God, hosting Singles Conferences, and mentoring other women. I was on fire for God and living purposefully, carrying this expectation for a career, and dreaming of what next God had in store for me. I was surrounded by people at school who appreciated me and supported me in ministry, and I was at peace with myself.

While in Kingston, unexpected doors began to open for ministry, and I began going places I didn't even know existed in my own country to spread the Gospel. I was preaching at open-air meetings for entire weeks, with classes in the mornings, and ministering at churches where I was invited to preach on Sundays. There were persons in my life who saw greatness was on me, and who kept on pushing and motivating me not to settle, but to soar like an eagle. I was proud of the woman I had become, and also proud of the fact that my past would no longer define me. I had also promised myself that I would steer clear of relationships and remain pure until marriage.

I was finally at peace with me. I was contented and I still had my job to return to after school. My daughter was growing up in a loving environment and I was experiencing joy unspeakable, but all this was about to be shattered by the unlikeliest person.

A year before I entered the seminary, I had become friends with a beautiful couple who I called my second parents. I met them while ministering consistently in a particular community. I was invited over to their house numerous times, and I spent many weekends with them. It was on one of these weekends that I met a man who I became so entangled with in a soul tie that was difficult for me to let go of. I became trapped in this web of a relationship based on a so-called prophetic word that I had received.

I recall one evening I went to a tent crusade in Ocho Rios, St. Ann where the speaker was someone of international renown. The experience would have a long-lasting impact on my life. The preacher came and took me out of my seat and told me that God had a word for me.

He proceeded to tell me that God was going to use me in extraordinary ways and that I would operate under the prophetic gift. He went further and indicated that I would meet my husband by my next birthday, and the key thing was that 'buildings surrounded him'. I was in a state of shock, pondering if this was real. "Is this man fake or could he really be hearing from God?"

As time passed, I went to spend a weekend with the couple, my second parents; and on one particular evening, we were seated having dinner together when the phone rang. My spiritual mother handed the phone to me, stating that her friend seemed to be in distress and wanted to speak to me about coming to pray for her son. The lady with whom I was staying dropped me off at the house and I prayed for the young man and left.

Two weeks later, the young man's mother called me at work to give me an update on him, then gave him the phone to speak with me. We connected that first day we spoke on the phone and a friendship developed between us. Another week came and I went again to spend the weekend with the couple, and this time I took a stroll, intending to visit the lady whose son I had prayed for.

She was not there, and I had chosen to walk an extended distance which caused my chest to tighten up because I was asthmatic. Her son saw that I was in distress and asked me to come and sit in his room and wait until I was strong enough to leave.

While waiting for my chest to relax, my eyes saw the most beautiful pencil drawing of a house on a stand, and I was moved to ask the man about it. He told me that he was the one who drew it and that this is what he does, being a draftsman. This encounter developed into a quick friendship which matriculated into a relationship, later leading to some dark moments of my life.

I cannot say how it happened, but over time we became inseparable. We spoke daily on the phone and he managed to weave himself into my heart. He was a single father and I was a single mother which is something we had in common, giving us common ground to speak. I didn't know what I had gotten myself into, but I was in over my head in this relationship.

My relationship with 'Bill' (not his real name) was becoming more demanding as each weekend I had to go home from school just to spend time with him and his son. I had many doubts in my head about our relationship because he told most of his family members that we were only friends. I felt as if he was ashamed of me, and even his mother saw me as his so-called best friend. I, however, kept letting these things slide, and kept convincing myself that everything would smooth out.

At times, things felt good, while other times things weren't what I expected them to be. Before long I found myself in a place that I had avoided for four years. I had not set up any boundaries, and I fell into the danger zone and ended up sleeping with him.

I had now hit rock bottom once more emotionally, and I began to wrestle with my conscience and the fact that I was a woman who was still preaching the Gospel of Jesus Christ.

People looked up to me and I had failed them because I

was unable to control my sexual desires. I want to be as transparent as possible and allow the world to know that as a leader I struggled with sexual purity. With this person the sexual encounter didn't happen on one occasion but became a habit. I tried to walk away from him by citing everything that was wrong with the relationship; however, that didn't work. I felt as though I couldn't leave him, and he had such a stronghold on me which I could not explain.

I was his little secret, and there was no way he could let his mother know that we were involved. One of the discoveries I made along the way was that his family, especially his parents, had an issue with me being full-figured.

Yes, I was and still am a full-figured woman. I also discovered that he was involved at the same time with another woman who lived in the United Kingdom. This wounded me even more, yet I still remained with him.

He did all he could to keep me with him, but I was too naïve because I loved him and his son, so I ensured that I was there for them both and went home every weekend. This cycle continued for quite some time, and before I knew it he was accepted into a course in Kingston and would end up staying with his aunt who lived only ten minutes walking distance from my school.

I strongly believed this was my test which I was failing quite miserably. Being at the Seminary was my avenue of escape, but what could I do now that he was in close proximity to me? I couldn't run, neither could I hide. He was a charmer and knew how to get what he wanted. When he started his program in Kingston, he became a familiar face on my school campus, and this brought us even closer to each other.

I eventually introduced him to my friends at school and also to those whom I lived with on the dormitory. He would come by quite often to visit me, and I guess he felt more at ease because he was not where his mother was. So, he devoted much of his time to me, and I continued to do random things for him as before. What I didn't realize was that others were observing our relationship and they were asking questions.

Many observed how much I loved and adored him, but for some reason he appeared to have been struggling with his feelings towards me. We argued and fought so much, and this took a toll on me emotionally.

Somehow, I knew that I was fighting a losing battle, but I kept telling myself that he was my husband, and I had gotten the prophetic word to prove that, so he would change eventually. I am so ashamed to confess this, but in all this time he never told me that he loved me. I told him on numerous occasions how much I loved him, and if I asked him if he did his response was, "If I didn't I wouldn't be spending this time talking to you."

I hated who I was becoming and felt trapped emotionally to a man who I believed was using me. I continued my educational program and the cycle with him continued; so, being tired and weary of him and how the relationship was one-sided, I began to ask others to earnestly help me pray about this situation.

I felt as if God had abandoned me and I was right back where I started. What was more damaging was that I continued to stand on different pulpits preaching the Word of God to others, I was wearing a mask and I prayed earnestly for God to expose me seeing that I was having trouble walking away.

When God Steps In

It so happened that in the summer of 2007 both of us went away on a student work program to the United States. It was frustrating that I stayed with my uncle and he stayed with his aunt, with only a twenty minutes journey separating us. I couldn't understand why things were playing out like this for me because, the more I wanted to get away from him, the more our paths seemed to be crossing.

Even though I felt as if God had abandoned me and I was walking contrary to His will, He always allowed me to see that He cared about me. While at my uncle's house I was introduced to a much older female who reached out to me to pray for her. I prayed for her and it eventually became a routine, forming a prayer line where we prayed every morning at 4:00 a.m.

It was through these early morning prayers that God intervened, and the Holy Spirit began to reveal things about the relationship that I was involved in, though it was not what I wanted to hear. I had a choice to make because I was being used by God but had an issue controlling my sexual addiction.

God showed up one morning on the line and declared that it was time for me to walk in freedom. That morning, one of the ladies began to pray – it was the same elderly lady that I had prayed for. She mentioned that today was the day of my deliverance. As she prayed for me, I felt the permeating power of the Holy Spirit infiltrating my mind, penetrating my soul. She told me that the Holy Spirit said that I should inhale and exhale three times. I did as I was instructed, but the third time she said, "You are going to breathe him out of your system."

I had no doubts because I had personally seen God move in some unconventional ways that brought deliverance to his people. That morning I felt different and free, and I took the initiative to call him and break off the relationship. He did not take it well and decided that he had to come and see me at my uncle's house.

Maybe he thought that if I saw him, I would go back on what I had said. However, when he came, I stood firm. He wanted us to have sex, but I told him that it won't happen. It was after much deliberation and perseverance that he realized that I was serious. It took me this trip to realize that he didn't love me as I had loved him. He was comfortable because I treated him like a king, in ways no other woman had treated him and his son before. I prayed that day, telling the Lord that what happened in New York shall stay there, and I intended to return home as a new woman. I kept my word and when I returned to Jamaica and to school, I slowly distanced myself from him and over time we were completely separated.

I no longer knew what was happening with him and I didn't care. I felt better about myself and was free to be me and spend time getting to know who I was. It was during this time that I started having a conversation with a young man who contacted me via the then-social media forum *Tagged*. We corresponded via that medium for a while, and as time progressed via Yahoo Messenger and email, and later exchanged phone numbers.

What was interesting about this turn of events was that he only lived fifteen minutes away from school. Eventually, we became friends and started getting to know each other. I was in no way ready for any relationship because I didn't want to see him as a rebound. I needed time to heal, as well as refocus on my relationship with God.

God, in His goodness and mercy, favoured me by placing three ladies in my life who became my spiritual support system until I completed my Studies, along with the persons who were already in my life but lived in the United States. Doors began to open in Kingston for ministry and I was now travelling to various communities doing crusades week after week. I became so busy with ministry and schoolwork that I had completely forgotten about Bill, nor did I want to engage in any more relationships. I found myself back at a place of peace with God and walking wholeheartedly in my purpose.

Encouragement

It doesn't matter how far you feel you have strayed from God; He is right there waiting to accept you back into His fold. It could be that you may be in a relationship like the one I spoke of and deep within you know it is one-sided. There is nothing wrong in walking away. Sometimes we hold on to these relationships, not out of desperation, but like me, you received a prophetic word about a person fitting that criteria. Yet after months and even years, things are not getting any better. Be strong and courageous and walk away!

As Christians we are not called to be perfect. We will fall, but each time we fall, we get back up and this time stronger than before. I fell so many times but by God's grace I got up. I didn't do it on my own.

CHAPTER 6
The Importance of Community

"No one person can fulfil all your needs. But the community can truly hold you. The community can let you experience the fact that, beyond your anguish, there are human hands that hold you and show you God's faithful love." —Henri Nouwen

As I settled on completing my degree and being involved in ministry, the three local women and the ones overseas became my actual support. Each week they met with me and we would pray together for hours, and one of the ladies in particular took me as her daughter. All three women were very close friends and study partners who were attending the Caribbean Graduate School of Theology and pursuing their master's degrees in psychology at the time.

The lady who took me under her wings not only supported me spiritually but ensured that I was never hungry. At the end of every month she would grocery shop for her household and for me, and brought the items to school for me. I didn't know what I did to deserve what she was doing for me, but I blessed God for what He was doing in my life.

God gave me a mother away from home. She would take me home with her on weekends, and I would accompany her as well to fasting services every Saturday at Portmore Missionary Church. She took great care of me and made sure that I had money at all times. I believe God was teaching me a valuable lesson here, that He was able to meet all my needs spiritually and physically.

God knows what we need and when we need it. I was at that place where God knew I needed these women who deposited in me the virtues that I would need later in my life. I recognized that with these women I could be vulnerable, not knowing that I would end up needing them more than ever as the temptation of my past with Bill came calling once more. I hid nothing from them. I was open to them about my feelings for Bill who had started to come back around.

One weekend I went home, and we had an encounter which led to us sleeping together again. I then remembered that I had a speaking engagement in the coming week and realized I couldn't do it. I had had enough of this and wanted this part of my life to be over. No matter how hard I tried I always ended up in the bed of fornication, and this time things had to change. I called the person who had extended the invitation to me and tried to cancel but it was too late.

That day I reached out to one of the three ladies who was a Pastor and I opened up about the act that I had indulged in. To be honest, I was not expecting the response I got. She told me that "all have sinned and fallen short of the glory of God" and who is she to condemn or judge me. She asked me

to turn to Romans 8, that I should read and meditate on it.
I've taken the liberty of sharing this passage in full here:

> There is no condemnation for those who belong to Christ Jesus,
> and because you belong to Him, the power of the life-giving Spirit
> has freed you from the power of sin that leads to death.
> The Law of Moses was unable to save us because of the weakness
> of our sinful nature. So, God did what the law could not do. He
> sent his own Son in a body like the bodies we sinners have. And in
> that body, God declared an end to sin's control over us by giving
> his Son as a sacrifice for our sins. He did this so that the just
> requirement of the law would be fully satisfied for us, who no
> longer follow our sinful nature but instead follow the Spirit. Those
> who are dominated by the sinful nature think about sinful things,
> but those who are controlled by the Holy Spirit think about things
> that please the Spirit.
> So letting your sinful nature control your mind leads to death.
> But letting the Spirit control your mind leads to life and peace. For
> the sinful nature is always hostile to God. It never did obey God's
> laws, and it never will. That's why those who are still under the
> control of their sinful nature can never please God. But you are not
> controlled by your sinful nature. You are controlled by the Spirit if
> you have the Spirit of God living in you.
> (And remember that those who do not have the Spirit of Christ
> living in them do not belong to him at all.) And Christ lives within
> you, so even though your body will die because of sin, the Spirit
> gives your life because you have been made right with God. The
> Spirit of God, who raised Jesus from the dead, lives in you. And
> just as God raised Christ Jesus from the dead, he will give life to
> your mortal bodies by this same Spirit living within you.
> Therefore, dear brothers and sisters, you have no obligation to
> do what your sinful nature urges you to do. For if you live by its
> dictates, you will die. But if through the power of the Spirit you put

to death the deeds of your sinful nature, you will live. For all who are led by the Spirit of God are children of God. So you have not received a spirit that makes you fearful slaves. Instead, you received God's Spirit when he adopted you as his own children. Now we call him, "Abba, Father." For his, Spirit joins with our spirit to affirm that we are God's children. And since we are his children, we are his heirs. In fact, together with Christ, we are heirs of God's glory. But if we are to share his glory, we must also share his suffering. Yet what we suffer now is nothing compared to the glory he will reveal to us later. For all creation is waiting eagerly for that future day when God will reveal who his children really are. Against its will, all creation was subjected to God's curse. But with eager hope, the creation looks forward to the day when it will join God's children in glorious freedom from death and decay. For we know that all creation has been groaning as in the pains of childbirth right up to the present time. And we believers also groan, even though we have the Holy Spirit within us as a foretaste of future glory, for we long for our bodies to be released from sin and suffering.

We, too, wait with eager hope for the day when God will give us our full rights as his adopted children, including the new bodies he has promised us. We were given this hope when we were saved. (If we already have something, we don't need to hope for it. But if we look forward to something we don't yet have, we must wait patiently and confidently. And the Holy Spirit helps us in our weakness. For example, we don't know what God wants us to pray for. But the Holy Spirit prays for us with groanings that cannot be expressed in words. And the Father who knows all hearts knows what the Spirit is saying, for the Spirit pleads for us believers in harmony with God's own will. And we know that God causes everything to work together[m] for the good of those who love God and are called according to his purpose for them. For God knew his people in advance, and he chose them to become like his Son so that his Son would be the firstborn among many brothers and sisters. And having chosen them, he called them to come to him. And having called them, he gave them right standing with himself. And having given them right standing, he gave them his glory.

What shall we say about such wonderful things as these? If God is for us, who can ever be against us? Since he did not spare even his own Son but gave him up for us all, won't he also give us everything else? Who dares accuse us whom God has chosen for his own? No one—for God himself has given us right standing with himself. Who then will condemn us? No one—for Christ Jesus died for us and was raised to life for us, and he is sitting in the place of honour at God's right hand, pleading for us Can anything ever separate us from Christ's love?

Does it mean he no longer loves us if we have trouble or calamity, or are persecuted, or hungry, or destitute, or in danger, or threatened with death? (As the Scriptures say, "For your sake we are killed every day; we are being slaughtered like sheep." No, despite all these things, overwhelming victory is ours through Christ, who loved us and I am convinced that nothing can ever separate us from God's love. Neither death nor life, neither angels nor demons, neither our fears for today nor our worries about tomorrow—not even the powers of hell can separate us from God's love. No power in the sky above or in the earth below—indeed, nothing in all creation will ever be able to separate us from the love of God that is revealed in Christ Jesus our Lord." (Romans 8:1-38, NLT).

Get Back Up Again

I chose to quote the entire chapter so that you too can read what the Word of God is saying to you right now. You may have "fallen from grace" as I did; maybe it is not of a sexual nature, but at some point in your walk with the Lord, you have messed up. **Press**, **Push**, and **Persevere**. God will not abandon you no matter the state you are in. Look around and examine your circle.

Are you able to be vulnerable with those in your circle? Are they uplifting you and encouraging you to pursue your dreams and visions? If not, maybe it's time to let go of these people and ask God to send the right people into your life who will help you to walk the path he has chosen for you.

I command you to STOP right now and shut down every negative thought that is wrestling with you in your mind that God is no longer with you. That is a lie that I believed until I began to soak my thoughts in this chapter of Romans. Yes, you have messed up and, in your estimation, it is extremely bad, but God shall turn this your mess into a testimony. Hallelujah!!!

I pray for you right now, "Lord Jesus, I thank you for all the messes that have happened in the life of your son/daughter because it has humbled them and is preparing them to be a living witness and testimony to others who themselves have messed up, and are on the verge of giving up. Help them to learn from these experiences and grow stronger in You. In Jesus name, Amen!"

Overcoming the Bondage of Sexual Sin

After reading the text, I was still adamant that I couldn't go to the church and stand on the platform to minister. The pastor encouraged me to repent and allow her some time to pray about the matter. I did as I was instructed, crying out to the Lord in repentance and fasting, asking God, "When will this particular pattern stop happening to me?"

In the week following she got back to me and told me to go ahead and minister at the event. She proceeded to tell me that God has a purpose for me and that one day I will overcome this, and it will be a part of my testimony of God's grace in my life. Now, here I am today sharing these intimate details with you of how I struggled with sexual sin as a minister, but it's true that I'm able to do so because God raised up women and men who stood by me and helped me fight the battle on their knees.

These women became my accountability partners who I had to give true accounts to, and they kept me grounded. All this time, I was fasting, praying and doing it on my own with great expectation that one day I would become strong enough to resist the temptation. It wasn't until I became vulnerable about this struggle and began to speak to my prayer mothers that I began to experience true freedom. I no longer wanted to keep it a secret out of fear of being judged and condemned. I needed to be free to worship God in the beauty of holiness, without the guilt of fornication. They loved me through it all and gave me a different view of how God sees us through grace.

To concretize this point, I needed to be set free from the bondage of fornication. I recall going into the beautiful hills of St. Andrew to a place called Mavis Bank, to minister at a week of revival. That day in particular, as I stood on the platform ministering, a little girl who was seated next to a man came to my side. Every move I made, she made as well. I couldn't understand it, but I decided that I would not be distracted.

I felt as if she was there to strengthen me because as I preached, she worshipped at my side, and was just asking the Lord to bless me. After the service, a man who was introduced to me as an Evangelist walked over to me and told me the Holy Spirit gave him a command and a word to give to me. He said that as I was ministering, the Holy Spirit told him that he and his wife should pray over my life daily until God blessed me with a husband.

He proceeded to tell me that the enemy was trying to use the sexual sin of fornication to keep me in bondage. I was shocked! He continued to tell me that as long as I continued in that act, I would never experience the fullness of what God called me to do. I wept openly because here was a stranger, a man I never knew, whom I met for the very first time, speaking from the mouth of God, and what he said was indeed the truth.

From that day until today, as I sit writing this book, this Minister and his wife have not only kept their obedience to this word, but are still in constant support in my life and ministry.

God was showing up big time and causing me to realize that He was serious about me walking in His perfect will, and as such was sending me help in the form of human beings who were serious about seeing me accomplish my God-given purpose on the earth. I left the revival with a renewed hope and faith that God was working on my behalf, and that He had placed people in my life to help me succeed.

Maybe you, too, are struggling with an area that you have prayed and fasted about consistently, but it appears as if God is not hearing you. I implore you: don't give up; the answer is on its way. Maybe the answer may not come in the way you expect it, but be open to the fact that God speaks in mysterious ways. At this moment He is telling you that this struggle is not meant to destroy you, and you shall overcome.

Let yourself loose by releasing that which you have been holding on to that has kept you in bondage. It could be sexual sin, various types of abuse, or it may be that you had an abortion and the shame of it has held you in captivity. Right now, I invite you to inhale and exhale three times and at the end of the third round say, "Lord Jesus, I am letting go of this. No longer will I allow it to keep me in bondage. In Jesus Name, Amen."

Broken but Not Forsaken

After walking in freedom for months, Bill came in search of me and we started to correspond again, but this time I knew my boundaries and held firm to them. He realized that I was serious about the separation. He tried to prey on my emotions, but I was unmovable. I was no longer a naïve woman and I knew that he didn't love me. I knew how I felt about him, and God knew the love was not going to die anytime soon.

One day he called me on the phone and said he wanted to speak to me in person about something, and he would also like for us to see a counsellor together. I was floored because I was wondering why we needed to see a counsellor. However, I made an appointment with the school counsellor.

I felt uneasy so my next move was to engage God in prayer and fasting the Monday before the meeting. I fasted all day and night shut up in my dormitory room, seeking God earnestly about this meeting. In the wee hours of the morning, God gave me a vision which was very clear, but I could not comprehend how it would play out; nonetheless, I committed the meeting to God.

During the session, the counsellor asked him to speak first and he began telling her how much he appreciated me, and how I have cared for his son. He proclaimed that there are times that he did not do things to show me how much he cared, but he did and wanted me to know that. When it was my time to speak, I confronted him about his treatment of me, and the fact that the relationship had always been one-sided, how he pretended with everyone that we were just friends and nothing more, when he knew without a doubt that we had been involved in an intimate relationship for three and a half years.

He said he wanted a second chance to show me that he really cared for me, but I was innocent to the fact that I was being set up in such a way that I would be broken to the point of severe depression. The end result was that on the same day of the counselling session, I found out later from a close mutual friend of ours that he was getting married. I was in disbelief!

My friend had called to find out what was happening because she knew we were together. She wanted to know how and when did this new relationship develop since he and I were always together. I was played and played big time! She said that she had to call me to find out what was going on, but in the end, she realized that I was clueless about this.

It went even further than that: he kept corresponding with me and pretended as if everything was normal until I confronted him. At first, he denied being married, but when I told him the name of the woman and the location of the wedding, he knew I had legitimate information. I was done, humiliated, played and disgraced. I shared the most intimate parts of me with him while at the same time compromising my relationship with God for a man that I believed with all my heart was destined to be my husband, who had now proven to have only been using and manipulating me.

I grieved long and hard. I cried for days, weeks and months, leading into years.

I share this story with you to echo the fact that it was the community of these praying women and men, along with my parents, who helped me through this dark period of my life. There were days when I couldn't study, eat, nor sleep. I cried through some of my classes because I couldn't process what was happening to me.

Bill still had the audacity to be calling me wanting to talk, but I was out of it. The word I had held onto all these years was not true. "How could He do this to me? How could God allow this to happen to me?"

My prayer mothers never relented, neither did my parents nor my closest schoolmates who knew the intimate details of my life. They prayed for me and encouraged me not only in the Word, but took me out to dinners and other events in an attempt to pull me out of the depression.

During this time, I became very weary with what is considered the prophetic, especially *words of knowledge* that had to do with a person's personal life. I, too, operated under the prophetic gift, and for that reason I held back many times when ministering because I didn't want anyone to get hurt like I was on account of a prophecy.

Encouragement

Christianity cannot be lived in isolation—we need community. A community offers us hope and support as we walk through some of the darkest moments of our lives. Stop right now! You have read the chapter. Reflect on those in your life who have been there for you in your deepest and darkest moments and begin to thank God for them.

Even when you feel alone as if no one is there, God remains constant and continues to work to set you free. It could be that at this moment you might be facing a storm, a period of intense hurt and pain due to past events, but God has raised up people who will pray for you and petition Him on your behalf.

Be open to the fact that in order to overcome these moments, you will have to open your mouth and speak about it. Share with someone what you are experiencing, and watch God bring healing to you through community. Open up and become accountable to someone as you walk this Christian path, and you will be amazed at the healing you will experience while in community.

God has people reserved who understand His grace and will not judge nor condemn you, but love you through your pains and scars. These women and men of God surrounded me not only with prayer, but with love which caused me not to give up; and restored my hope and faith in Christ Jesus.

Is there a man or woman in your past right now that you are holding on to that you believe was meant to be yours? Will you let him/her go and allow God's will to be done in you? I pray that even now.

May God send you persons who will be your accountability partners, who will bear you up in love and prayer. You and I may have been broken but we were never forsaken. May the Holy Spirit restore the broken pieces of your life that were damaged through intimate relationships. Amen.

CHAPTER 7
Cleaning House: Acceptance and Forgiveness

"If you offend, ask for pardon; if offended forgive."
—Ethiopian Proverb

I shared in the previous chapters some issues that messed me up emotionally and mentally over the years that were constant sources of struggle. These issues from my past scarred me so badly that I was unable to receive any form of love from others. I had issues with loving myself and allowing others to love me, which drove me to settle for less. I feared entering relationships because I had this preconceived notion that all men were the same, and refused to allow anyone to enter my space unless I wanted it to happen. I saw myself for years as a victim - a victim of my circumstances, and as a result I became hardened.

I was now an established and ordained evangelist going all over Jamaica and the United States preaching the Gospel on many different platforms. People all over knew my name and I kept hearing how anointed I was, and how one could see the hand of God on me. Yet! No one had a clue about the demons that I had been wrestling with. These demons haunted me so much that there were times when I didn't believe that I was supposed to be doing anything for God.

I wrestled with my sexual appetite as a woman of God who others held in high esteem. It didn't matter how much I fasted and prayed, it would still happen, and I was tired of it. And yet deliverance had come! I discovered the wonderful power of God's grace and love. His love for me was unconditional and broke down every barrier that the enemy had set up. I was living no longer in shame because he had turned my mourning into dancing.

I finally walked with my head held up like a woman on a mission, with the attitude of an overcomer, and the voice of a lioness. What was meant to destroy me was now a testimony of God's grace and unending love for me.

I can unreservedly say that I never heard my parents telling me as a child growing up the three essential three words, "I love you" either to me or to each other. Love is something that can bring a revival within the soul of man which brings about healing. Love is a central theme that runs throughout the Scriptures, and it was love for humanity that led Jesus to die on the cross for us.

Getting Past My Past

My dilemma was that I couldn't get past my past, and this was because I was struggling with forgiveness. The only way for me to walk in freedom was to look back in order to look forward. What I mean by this is that as I began to reflect on all the things I had faced from my childhood and how they had scarred me, I realized I needed to let it go.

I wrestled a lot with God, asking, "Why me?" Why did He allow all the evil things to happen to me? The sexual abuse that I suffered led to my becoming quite promiscuous, so much that one day I reached breaking point, and realized that I had messed up so many times that I was unable to breathe. I never knew my life would turn out to be like this; and even though God was using me as His vessel, I felt unclean almost all the time.

I pressed and pushed and sought the Lord for freedom, and what He revealed via the Holy Spirit was that I first needed to accept the things that happened, and in so doing I embraced what the Apostle Paul said wholeheartedly in 1 Thessalonians 5:18, "In everything give thanks; for this is the will of God in Christ Jesus for you" (NKJV).

On this particular day, I fully surrendered my heart, will and everything to God and worshipped Him by accepting all the bad things that had happened to me over the years. My heart's focus on self-pity, anger, and bitterness shifted to one of thanksgiving. I began to thank God for everything that had happened to me: the rape, sexual abuse, the ill-treatment meted out to me by my stepmother, and the neglect and abandonment I faced as a child that accompanied me into adulthood. I found myself calling people by their names and saying, "I forgive you". I was cleaning my house, my heart where the Holy Spirit dwells.

Many times we wrestle with things of the past because we fail to resolve within ourselves that they happened to us. We often find it difficult to accept what these persons did to us, and we hold on to the hurt and pain because we believe we deserve some answers. I did the same, but the answers never came. Once I began to accept that this was my reality, I began to experience something anew happening within me.

You and I cannot change what has happened in the past – some of the circumstances we had control over and some we did not. However, acceptance is key to our moving forward. It may be difficult to accept that these things happened, especially when you know those who were the major contributors to your pain. But God is able to help you. God knows what concerns us and the issues we face are not a surprise to Him.

As we accept our scars and those who played a part in them, only then will we be able to move on to that next phase of our life. After I went through this process of acceptance, I was able to move on to forgiving those who had wronged me, and I felt a great burden lift off my shoulders.

Transformation

After accepting and forgiving my wrongdoers, the relationship with my stepmother was not only healed by the power of forgiveness, but we became inseparable. I have grown to love and appreciate her. God allowed me to understand that her actions were as a result of her brokenness, of being abused as a child by the one who was supposed to be her protector, her father. She didn't know better and couldn't stand the thought of seeing a father love his daughter the way my father loved me.

God, through the Holy Spirit, brought healing to her, as well as to our relationship. She was able to share in the glorious moment of seeing God's will manifest in my life. There were moments when she could not get past what she had done, but I reassured her that God has forgiven her. There was no need to walk around feeling guilty and as I had also forgiven her, she now needed to forgive herself.

God also began to work on my entire family as I surrendered to Him and exercised the gift of forgiveness. Today, my mother and stepmother are very close friends. My mother and I are even closer than before. My stepfather and I have developed a bond with each other, and my father is very much aware of all that I had experienced in the past. This was as a result of the Holy Spirit working through me to begin the process of restoration in my family.

My first real ministry was to my household. I had to be a living testimony to what I was preaching. I confess that it was not an easy task but over time it got a bit easier to do. I became a free woman walking in the liberty by which Jesus Christ had set me free. I was no longer a slave to unforgiveness. Ministry took on greater meaning, and as I ministered to people, the Lord began to challenge me to share portions of my story.

One of the most challenging things that I have come to

realize is that your family oftentimes never see you as transformed; it takes time and the work of the Holy Spirit to open their eyes to the transformation. This was what happened in my case because many thought I would never have made it this far in my Christian faith. My father who is a backslider would tell me that numerous people came up to him and told him how I was being used by God to impact their lives. Other family members were also reaching out to me, requesting that I pray for them. God had started something in my life, and He would see it through to completion.

The years passed and I grew more and more in my faith, and I continued to witness verbally to my family and try my endeavour best to live out my faith for them to see God through my life. As I penned this chapter, I felt fresh waves of emotions sweep over me and I couldn't help it but to shed some tears. I was not bitterly looking back at the negative things that had happened to me. Oh, how faithful God has been since I opened my heart to Him. Relationships are important whether they are family, spousal, or even friendships; and what I had longed for concerning relationships, God was already working on.

Today, I value the relationship I have with my stepmother and I have become the daughter she never had. I truly am honoured that God did what man could not do. He restored us to a place where we can love each other without looking back at what happened in the past. I am also at a place where

I have had healthy interactions with my cousins who had offended me, and I've embraced them with much love.

There is an old Jamaican adage which states that, *who knows better should do better*' and this I have incorporated in my journey. I know better because I am a child of God and I have a responsibility to walk according to the Word of God. Each day brings with it new challenges. Maybe today is your new day to embrace that you cannot change the struggles that you have undergone in your past, but you certainly can change your future response. God's love has been poured out into us in such a way that it does not come with reservations but is unconditional.

Encouragement

Today, I encourage you to take up the challenge and allow the Holy Spirit to help you to love those who have wronged you. Jesus commands us "... forgive others, and you will be forgiven" (Luke 6:37). I know that you might be questioning my sanity at this point, but trust me when I say that I know that forgiveness is never an easy task, but it is doable. Yes, I know it is not easy and causes waves of emotions, bad memories, and even pain that you may have locked away somewhere in your heart.

Nonetheless, the time is now to face those challenges and allow the Holy Spirit to begin the healing process in your life. Forgiveness is a universal struggle that many Christians share in common with those of the secular world. However, the difference is that we have Jesus Christ Who will help us in times of need.

Another famous saying, I hear is, "Rev., I forgive but I will not forget." This implies that persons will forgive with their lips, but never with their hearts. We will not remind persons of what they have done to us in the past, nor will we use the past against them, but this is not the essence of forgiveness that God requires of us. I, too, was guilty of saying the same thing, until I understood that when I forgive others, I too will be forgiven. The Apostle Paul mentions that "...love keeps no record of wrongs" (1 Corinthians 13:5 NIV).

In the same instance, I know that when we ask God to forgive us, He does not hold up our history before Him each time we go before Him seeking pardon. He forgives us and so it must be with us that when we forgive, we should not keep a record of the wrong, but ask the Holy Spirit to help us to move beyond it and embrace the person/s wholeheartedly as if they had not wronged us. Forgiveness flows from a heart that is baptized with the unconditional love of Christ. When you and I surrender to God's love, He in turn will teach us how to love others unconditionally. Right at this moment, let us pray.

Prayer

Lord Jesus, I pray for the one that is reading this chapter and struggling with unforgiveness. May your Holy Spirit help this person to let go of those that caused offence and begin the process of healing in his/her life. I also pray for the ones who may be in need of forgiveness. May the Holy Spirit release them from the guilt carried over the years due to what they have done. I speak the peace of our Lord and Saviour Jesus Christ over every heart and mind right now, as this person surrenders to the power of the Holy Spirit's work in his/her life. Amen.

CHAPTER 8
The Better Part

"God does not give us overcoming life; He gives us life as we overcome." —Oswald Chambers

The prophet Isaiah writes in chapter 55:8-9, "My thoughts are nothing like your thoughts," says the Lord. And my ways are far beyond anything you could imagine. For just as the heavens are higher than the earth, so my ways are higher than your ways and my thoughts higher than your thoughts" (NLT). I can attest to the fact that what I thought about myself was nothing compared to what God had in His thoughts and mind for me.

My life began to take on new dimensions – mark you, I still had struggles, but I was now a confident woman. I was more purpose-driven and goal-oriented. I had a lot going on for me. Ministry kept me busy, I had completed my first degree and my daughter was now in high school. After completing the degree in Social Work, I went back to my government job and was relocated to work in the parish of St. Mary as a Social Worker in the Child and Adolescent Mental Health department, a job that I became passionate about.

I had no idea that I would have ended up loving this profession as I do now. I initially wanted to pursue law and I worked hard at it, but God had another plan. It was His clear direction I had adhered to when I sent in my application to the Jamaica Theological Seminary. This vocation opened so many doors for me to connect with other professionals, children, and parents. God gave me the opportunity to speak into the lives of others and this was more fulfilling to me than anything else. I also faced situations on the job that conflicted with my past, but I was able to use the scars that I faced to show empathy to others, and effectively help those who too struggled with sexual abuse and rape.

I became an advocate for those who were 'closet children' like myself, and were victims of others. My determination and drive catapulted me to begin to receive invitations to speak at graduations throughout the parish of St. Mary, and before I realized it, I was the keynote speaker at many events involving Parent-Teacher Associations, the Jamaica Constabulary Force and other institutions that invited me to speak.

At one point I had to look in the mirror and say, "God, is this truly the timid little girl who thought she would have amounted to nothing, now speaking on platforms to different age groups and impacting lives while being vulnerable?" I also began to comprehend the reason why the Lord led me to become a Social Worker. My brokenness was the means by which I would be able to have compassion for others, and which gave me the ability to empathize with them.

I often say to myself, "Self, if you had never been broken, how could you truly minister to the broken?" Talk comes easy, but when you have been through something it allows you to make a connection to someone who has had similar experiences. People desire to hear from others who have been through some storms and have overcome. In so doing, it becomes easier for them to work at navigating their way through the hard times.

Naked and Not Ashamed

I had learned to become vulnerable over the years, and each time I went to speak on any forum I was open to the leading of the Holy Spirit. If God said, "It's time to be real," I shared a part of my story. I recall the Child and Mental Health team was asked to facilitate a two-day teacher's workshop. My supervisor asked me if I could share on the topic of "Dealing with Your Mental Health." I was happy to facilitate this segment.

On the day I began to do the presentation that I had so diligently prepared, the Holy Spirit nudged me to share my experience of sexual abuse and rape. One of the questions I explored was, "Are there any skeletons in your closet that is prohibiting you from experiencing good mental health?"

While narrating this period of darkness in my life, my eyes shifted to an older woman who sat at the back of the classroom, and I saw tears continuously running down her face openly.

I was tempted to stop sharing but the Lord kept prompting me to continue, and I shared how for years I was affected by these traumatic events, and how I was able to overcome these battles. I proceeded to ask if there was anyone that needed me to pray for them and a few teachers came forward, the older lady among them. Before I could open my mouth, she asked if I could give her permission to share which I did. What the woman shared had me in total awe: she said that for more than twenty years she had been living with a secret and it had stolen so much from her.

She shared that she had been raped by a family friend which resulted in her becoming pregnant at a young age. She was brought up in the church and had faced a lot of condemnation and judgement because she carried the pregnancy as an unmarried woman. She kept the identity of the person as a secret and had registered the child in her name. She was afraid no one would believe her because the man was her fathers' friend and much older than her. She wept bitterly and disclosed that this was the first time she was sharing the experience, and that for years she kept telling her daughter that her father was dead.

Her testimony led other women to open up and share their scars and how it impacted them and their relationships. I was happy that I had followed the leading of the Holy Spirit, and those women were able to begin the healing process while getting on the road to experiencing freedom and practicing good mental health. I was no longer afraid to share the scars that had made me into the woman I am today.

My life experiences were bitter, but they gave me something in common with many who are broken. God knew that what I was carrying inside, and that there would be many who needed to hear what I had been through. I had no more shame, and God had given me the boldness I needed to share my story of pain.

One thing I did as a mother was to teach my daughter from the age of two the importance of good touch and bad touch. I didn't care who it was: whether father, sister, brother, etc., she needed to let me know as soon as possible if she was touched in any way that made her uncomfortable.

When she grew older and was at an age where she could understand, I shared my story with her. I remember her crying and saying, "Mommy, you really went through all of this?" She blessed my heart when she told me how proud she was of me. I had a female professor at Jamaica Theological Seminary who taught me how to become naked and not ashamed in a Grief Counselling course.

She gave us an assignment on grief that allowed us to become vulnerable. At first I didn't know what to write, but after much prayer the Holy Spirit impressed on my heart to share my story of how I was robbed of my innocence (and innocence doesn't only mean your virginity) by being violated by my cousins, the experience of rape, and the inability of not being able to be my authentic self as a child.

As I wrote that paper, I grieved those moments that opened the door to shame, anger, inferiority, and bitterness; but it was also a moment of release for me as I shared what was inside my inner being. The next week of class, the lecturer shared that there was a paper that really touched her, and she shared snippets of it. Lo and behold, it was my paper. Her response empowered me to let go of all the negative emotions, embrace what was, and let what had happen become a stepping stone to impact others.

The One for Me

I was scared that no man would want me if they heard my story. I recall in 2010, I was in my office sitting at my desk when I heard the Holy Spirit speak clearly that my status was about to change. I smiled within myself and said, "Ok, Lord. Do as you wish." That day my stepmother called me on the phone and I shared the revelation with her, suggesting that my status could change either relationally or by naturalization.

Moreover, I was single at the time and quite comfortable with that too. If you recall, earlier I told you that during my tenure in the Seminary, I had the opportunity of corresponding with a young man I had met online on the platform called "Tagged." We became friends and it was at a time when I was an emotional wreck. He lived only fifteen minutes' drive away from the Seminary, and he had a co-worker who was attending the school as well.

I remember one day his co-worker approached me and asked when did Dave and I plan on getting married. I laughed and my response was, "I don't know about that". He was forthright in making me understand that Dave was a good man and I would not regret that decision. I was not there emotionally with Dave even though he expressed an interest before, but I was too afraid to open up to a man for a relationship. Dave and I met in person a few months after when I invited him to a production that I was a part of in Seminary.

He honoured me by keeping his promise to come, and that day another schoolmate of mine asked if he was my significant other. I was quick to dismiss this notion, but she exclaimed, "You guys look great together." Over time, we became very close friends and went out four times during my time at the Seminary. He was a breath of fresh air: he respected my boundaries, listened, and most of all I was able to be my true self around him. He knew about my last relationship and how that had worked out. He told me about his last relationship, and for that I had the utmost respect for him. When it was time to graduate, I invited him to my graduation and introduced him to my daughter and family who readily accepted him.

I returned home and we corresponded on rare occasions, but as fate would have it, I needed someone to help my daughter with Mathematics, and he was the one who I reached out to. His kind gesture cost him a lot in phone bills which escalated because he was diligent in helping her, and over time they bonded. Their bond and his approach to her warmed my heart, and the phone calls began to increase between us.

I must admit that he remained constant in my daughter's life, and she made sure to follow his advice even in her choice for high school. Eventually, he became my husband, but the decision was not made just like that. I had opened up about our relationship to the older women in my life who helped to pray me through this decision. I also introduced them to him and they, in turn, spoke with him on separate occasions.

Today, when others see us together, especially when I go out to minister, people ask me about this wonderful man that stands at my side in ministry. I share my story of how we met each other. Some are shocked when I say that I met my husband online, and that at first I was not in any way attracted to him. I must be transparent in sharing about my husband and how I conducted myself when he declared his intentions toward me. I could not see yet that God had destined us to be together. In my eyes, he was not the one for me.

I recall one day I went to the United States for ministry, and I had told him that for the two weeks I would be away that he needed to get his act together to decide what he wanted. While I was in Connecticut, he kept the connection between us going via Social Media. Believe me, I found that I couldn't restrain myself from constantly thinking about him.

After I had finished ministering, the women of God surrounded me and began to pray for me. One in particular told me to sit in a chair while another anointed me, and the other washed my feet. I was given a prophetic word and demonstration that marriage was upon me immediately. I was told to extend my hand and metaphorically told, "Take the baby boy from your hand." I was absolutely blown away by this manifestation of the Holy Spirit.

Later that day, one of the ladies, who was in her seventies, called me and asked in front of the other two women. "I heard the word of knowledge about marriage being upon you and this is immediate, so who is that young man?" I quickly defended myself by indicating that I was not involved in a relationship. The other sister shouted, "What about Dave?" I instantly shut that down by stating that he is just my friend and not my type.

You see, my eyes were blinded by my own desires of what I wanted in a man and what I thought was best for me. I was used to men being attracted to me who were slimmer, and Dave was on the heavier side. I had a problem with his image because I had a problem with mine, and I wrestled with what others were going to say about him, not looking at the character of this young man.

I was broken due to low self-esteem, and not knowing my worth trampled on his ego. I made sure to tell him that if we were ever to get married, he needed to lose weight because I didn't need any *fat* man in my life. Worst of all I was *fat* too! I could not find any concrete answers to give these mothers of Zion, and they rebuked me for what I had said and done. I went into fasting the next day and shut myself up in a room, pouring out all my heart to God.

I repented for the harsh words I had said to him, but even then, he didn't relent in his interest. His answer was, "Ok. I will lose the weight." These women of God helped me to see what I could not see through prayer and wise counsel. He proposed a year later and I said "Yes". I look back many times and smile because I almost let my past ruin what God had in store for me relationship-wise.

Walking in God's Plan for Me

On our wedding day, April 30, 2011, family and friends were present to witness this God-ordained event, which was by itself a testimony. I must say that my husband had lost 30 pounds and I didn't lose anything. This action of his taught me something about his character; and even though he didn't do it to please me, he showed me that he would do what he had to because he believed that God had put us together. He didn't want to miss what God had in store for him.

Our wedding took place in the famous New York City, with God working one miracle after another. We were immensely blessed as the older women in my life, along with my stepmother, gave us the best wedding we could ever dream of. It was my stepmother who bought my beautiful wedding gown, and this was her way of showing me how much she really appreciated me as her daughter.

God used His people to do the entire wedding without it costing us anything except our plane fares from Jamaica. They took care of the venue, transportation, bridal party, rings, and honeymoon. We were just surprised moment by moment as the day approached. To date, I am happily married with three beautiful children and currently live in Edmonton, Alberta, Canada.

God gave me His best and I am certain of that! My husband stands with me one hundred percent in ministry, and this has always been his nature since the beginning of our relationship. God finally put an end to my sexual struggle by placing a man of great integrity and character to stand by my side, and I have never yet one day felt ashamed in being vulnerable with him. I want to note, however, that before I got married, God had helped me through the intervention of my mentors to practice self-control, thereby curbing my sexual appetite.

As I pen this chapter, I am in the country of Canada which God destined to be our new home. This was an absolute God-thing and believe me, God sends us where He wants us to be. I recall several instances where God spoke directly to me through dreams concerning Canada, as well as through others about Canada, and the plans He had for us here. I didn't know how it was going to happen, but God did honour His word and brought us here.

The transition was not an easy one as I left my full-time Government job, friends and family, to come to a country where I had no family and was a stranger, but God had it in His better part for me. Change is inevitable but never readily acceptable, and this is where I found myself. There were days in this new country when I felt abandoned by God because I was in a hard place, a place of depression. I felt displaced but God knew even before the foundation of the earth that He had this path laid out in Canada for us, and this involved ministry. I struggled with not doing what I lived, and that was evangelism; nor was I affiliated with any church as yet.

Nevertheless, my husband and I remained prayerful about this situation and God led us to our current church where I am currently ordained as a Reverend. I recognize that I was unable to hide, and neither could I remain complacent for too long, because God began to show me the purpose for relocating us to Canada, which was for ministry. God began to place people strategically in our lives, which began to lead us into the path He wanted us to take. God allowed me time to grieve and mourn the fact that I had left the known for the unknown, and today I have no regrets.

God not only gave us a church home that I am actively involved in, serving as the Junior Pastor to the Senior Pastor, but He commanded me to go back to school. Currently, I am pursuing a master's degree in Divinity. My mind still cannot fathom the awesomeness of God and how when we humble ourselves at His feet, He leads us into the paths that He has destined for us.

Many times, these are paths that one can only dream of; but when God gets access to our hearts and lives, He has a profound way of turning things around for our good and His glory. My journey started out beautifully when I was born, but over time as I grew up, I began to face various challenges through the different stages of my life – a life that was riddled with shame, abuse, rejection, unforgiveness, and purposelessness.

I have suffered much in the past and still do experience times of suffering; but I have come to a place where I have grasped that the Gospel of Christ requires a life of suffering. Just look at Jesus' Disciples! They, too, suffered persecution and rejection, and some were even martyred in the end. Yet they chose the better part—*a surrendered life in Christ.* Jesus himself chose the better part and that was to do His Father's will, which makes us, Dear Reader, privileged people.

I can look back and say that suffering is a major part of the journey of any disciple of Christ, and most of the time it is so unbearable, but it comes with a surrendered life. I have chosen the better part indeed which was when I said, "Yes" to Jesus, and completely surrendered my will to Him. I gave Him absolute control to do as He pleased with me. I had rebelled on many levels but in the end, His purpose for my life was greater than I could even imagine.

One thing that came forcefully to me was a revelation that was so daunting for me. I can recall when I was praying about my marriage (I had issues with submission), the Holy Spirit revealed to me that I have not yet learned how to fully submit to God, therefore, I would have problems in submitting to my husband.

The idea is this: submission comes with surrendering. Yes, I said it and I will say it again. When I surrendered to God in totality, I became submissive to Him and His will for my life, and this caused me to let go of my own will. I wrestled with this because, submission in the context in which I was taught meant that a man would walk over me. Submitting to God is surrendering to His authority in my life. Through this revelation, I was able to begin to submit to my husband's authority. When we submit to God's authority, we allow Him to do as He pleases in and through us although it may cause us great pain. But this life is not lived in isolation but in community. In community, others will have a need to hear our stories of suffering and how God brought us through.

The Surrendered Life

Today, I am living a surrendered life to God. Over and over I have been broken, battered, and worn out, but like Mary I always find myself at His feet (in His presence) where I am restored. When Mary sat at Jesus' feet, it was an act of surrender, which resulted in Jesus saying that she had chosen the better part. My better part came to fruition when I opened my heart to God. As I surrendered to His ultimate plan for my life, things began to shift significantly, and my life began to get better and better.

This solemn act of surrendering enabled me to experience the grace of God. Like Joshua in Zechariah 3:3-4, who was clothed in filthy garments, when the Angel of the Lord commanded those around him to remove the filthy clothes and clothe him with splendid robes, so it is in my life. God has removed all the filthy garments of shame, sexual abuse, rape, inferiority, abandonment, and rejection, and clothed me with His grace exemplified by love, forgiveness, self-confidence, submission, humility, self-control and perseverance.

In relaying my story to you in this chapter, I shared how my better part included a marriage to a man who was not really my type but was God's best; relocating to a new country; once more enjoying my passion of evangelism and being unexpectedly ordained as a Pastor; going back to school in order to rightly divide the Word of Truth like Timothy; and all this became possible when I completely submitted to God. By surrendering, I began to walk into the plans He had for my life.

Encouragement

Today, my story may be similar or even different from yours, but God still remains true to His Word. According to Psalm 138: 8, "The Lord will perfect that which concerns me; Your mercy, O Lord, endures forever; Do not forsake the works of Your hands" (NKJV). God has a plan for you, my reader, and this plan is your better part. For you to fully walk in this plan, it requires you to walk in submission by surrendering to God's authority in your life.

Maybe your better part may not include marriage, but if you are called to live a single life, live it to the glory of God. God is able to bring you to a place where He will use your failures, messes and scars to help restore others to a place of healing. If you are struggling right now with surrendering to

God wholeheartedly, I am here to encourage you. With all you have been through, and knowing that you are here and reading this chapter, means that God wants to hear you say, "Lord, I surrender to Your will and Your way."

Let God through the Holy Spirit help you to let go of all that has kept you from experiencing the better part. There is nothing wrong in having plans – I also make plans. However, are your plans in line with the plans of God for your life? Jesus prayed for the will of His Father to be done in His life, and I share that same sentiment with you today. I pray that the will of the Father be made manifest in your lives today as you submit to His authority.

Today, I am basking in a healthy and fruitful relationship with my family members who hurt me, and many of my family members have come to walk with the Lord through my ministry to them, and others over time will too. God is a restorer and has a better part awaiting us. Will you open yourself right now to this better part and let God rewrite your life story, allowing His perfect will to become one with yours?

I encourage you, dear reader, to pause this minute and reflect on where you currently are. If you can answer truthfully that you are where God wants you to be, then begin to praise Him for all that He has done for you and continues to do. But if you are struggling with being where God wants you to be and feel stuck at this point in your life, it's time to *let go and let God*. He wants you to experience the better part like Mary, and it entails Him using your life as a memoir for others to come to know Him.

Prayer

Heavenly Father, I stand in the gap for the person reading this book right now. May s/he be open to Your call to begin to experience the better part that You have for them. Lord Jesus, remove every filthy garment that has them in bondage by enveloping them in your grace. Clothe them, Holy Spirit, with the virtues that they need such as love, justice, peace, and perseverance, which will enable them to continue to fight the good fight of faith. In Jesus name, Amen!

CONCLUSION

As a pastor, I chose to share how my story of struggle with issues from my past led me to live as a scarlet woman. You read about how I was scarred by the ones who should have protected, loved and cared for me, but instead were used by the enemy to try and kill the purpose of God in me.

When I became a Christian, I believed that everything was now different because God had washed me clean, and life was good until I began to struggle with my past and keeping my body sexually pure. I was a bitter woman with so many issues and I didn't know how to deal with them. What sank me deeper into distress was my struggle with my identity, and most of all the sexual sin of fornication.

My victory came when God placed men and women in my life who became my accountability partners, and I was not afraid to be vulnerable with them. I was struggling with various issues and keeping them as secrets - all the time deceiving myself that I could do it on my own. I had fasted and prayed about my situation countless times, but I was unable to defeat this issue that had become a stronghold in my life. It wasn't until I became vulnerable and opened up about these particular struggles to the circle of godly women who God placed in my life, that I was able, with their help, to overcome. They didn't judge me but showed me what God's grace looks like in human form.

God turned my life around and healed me in a holistic way. It involved a process that entailed accepting all that had happened to me in my past, with an understanding that most of it was not my fault; and in the end, I had to forgive all those who had offended me. I was able to begin a new chapter of my life by forgiving others and letting go of past hurts and scars. This led to me being able to walk in liberty.

God's presence in my life was a big deal, and through the act of submission by surrendering to God wholeheartedly, He turned my life around and I began to experience **The Better Part**. This better part entailed sharing with you the story of how my struggles eventually led to me living a surrendered life in ministry. God's plans for me superseded my expectations, and as I began to walk in relationship with Him, His plans for me began to unfold.

Today, I am a Social Worker in a vocation God called me into, and registered with the Alberta College of Social Workers in Canada. I am an ordained Pastor, a motivational speaker, mother, wife, and a student who is currently completing a Masters in Divinity. All this has been made possible by God because He had a plan for my life, and that was inclusive of all my pains.

I still have struggles, but today I have tasted and seen that the Lord is good, and I pray that you, too, will experience the better part that comes in living a surrendered life. It is not a life that often brings material wealth and fame, but is often a life of suffering and service. I have chosen to be His disciple and you have seen in my story how God has brought me to a place of peace, hope, and joy.

I would not change anything about my story. Like Joseph, who was later elevated to the palace as Pharaoh's Governor, experiencing the better part that God had in store for him, God shall elevate you too as you surrender to Him and begin to experience the better part He has for you.

SEVEN DAYS OF REFLECTION ON *THE BETTER PART*

Day 1, Chapter One
The Closet Child

Use the space provided or a journal to document your answer to the instructions for self-reflection.

When you reflect on your childhood, what are some of your fondest memories? List them and offer up prayers of thanksgiving unto God. If these memories cause you to be unhappy, then it's time to face those fears of the past. Take the time to write them down and then release them to God in prayer. Today, be intentional and confront your childhood issues. It's possible that it may take you more than a day, but be open to the work of the Holy Spirit in your life as the issues surrounding your childhood come to the surface.

And the peace of God, which surpasses all understanding, will guard your hearts and your minds in Christ Jesus. Philippians 4:7 (ESV).

_____

_____

_____

Day 2, Chapter Two
Knocked Down by the Unexpected

Use the space provided or a journal to document your answer to the instructions for self-reflection.

a. Life has presented you with many expected challenges that have left you broken. You have tried all you can to live a normal life, but circumstances keep popping up causing you to feel as if you are unable to bear it. Today, when life sucks, what do you do? When you look back at your life, did you have control over some of life's challenges that you faced? Take the time right now and chart some of the hardest challenges that made you believe that life just sucks, then write a prayer to God releasing all these issues (Abba, I Am yours. Prayer Adapted from the *Ragamuffin Gospel* by Brennan Manning).

b. Have you experienced life changes that should bring you moments of happiness, yet because you have been a slave to your past and present circumstances you lose out due to conflicting inner turmoil? Maybe the door has opened to new relationships, but experiences from the past dampen your outlook of progressing forward. I challenge you to see the events as they are individually.

c. Rejoice and celebrate when you need to, even when it is hard, believing with all your heart that you deserve to be happy and be your best at all times. Take a moment to reflect and write down a few times you should have celebrated but refused to do so because of past experiences. Then celebrate, yes, right now. Laugh or cry if you must.

"Laughter is wine for the soul - laughter soft, or loud and deep, tinged through with seriousness - the hilarious declaration made by man that life is worth living." —Sean O'Casey

_____

_____

_____

_____

_____

Day 3, Chapters 3-4
Answering God's Call

Use the space provided or a journal to document your answer to the instructions for self-reflection.

Have you ever felt that you are worth more than you believe, and that deep down you can sense that God has called you for a purpose? What are the things that God is speaking to your heart to do that you have become reluctant to do? Today is your day to ponder on these things prayerfully. Then be bold and answer God's call to be who He has called you to be.

"Trust in the Lord with all your heart and lean not on your own understanding; in all your ways submit to him, and he will make your paths straight." (Prov. 3:5-6, (NIV)

_____

_____

_____

_____

_____

_____

Day 4, Chapter 5
The Battle for Purpose

Use the space provided or a journal to document your answer to the instructions for self-reflection.

Have you often felt as if your life has no meaning or that it is purposeless? Does it seem as if nothing good has come your way and you are tired of settling for less? God has a purpose for you. Your destiny may seem delayed, but it is not denied. It is time to contend with the enemy for your destiny.

Fight this battle through prayer by making daily declarations from the word of God. Speaking them daily over your life, and trust God who will cause them to manifest. I have written the first one now so you can write the other six (6) and daily declare them over your life.

I declare that I am an overcomer by the blood of the Lamb and by the word of my testimony.

"For the revelation awaits an appointed time; it speaks of the end and will not prove false. Though it lingers, wait for it; it will certainly come and will not delay" (Habakkuk 2:3, NIV).

Day 5, Chapter 6
The Importance of Community

Use the space provided or a journal to document your answer to the instructions for self-reflection.

Communities are an excellent means of survival. We were never meant to be alone and that is why when God made Adam and gave him Eve as a wife. People are important and they help us along our journey. You may have been hurt by others in the past, but do not let this hinder you from experiencing the joy that others may contribute to you in times of great need.

Is there anyone in your life whom you see as a mentor or a spiritual help? Our spiritual life can never be lived in isolation; we need each other. Write down one or two names of persons you know, based on their Christian principles, character, and lifestyle, that may be good mentors and spiritual advisors for you. Be prayerful, then approach them and let them know where you are at spiritually, emotionally or otherwise, and tell them of the help you need.

"A friend loves at all times, and a brother is born for a time of adversity" (Prov. 17:17 NIV).

Day 6, Chapter 7

Cleaning House: Acceptance and Forgiveness

Use the space provided or a journal to document your answer to the instructions for self-reflection.

It is often a great struggle to accept that people have hurt us, whether in the past or present. Oftentimes it goes on for months and even years and we try to figure out why this person/s did what they did, and to no avail can we ever get the answers we seek. I encourage you today to try and accept what had happened to you, so you can once and for all let go of the past issues and progress towards the future.

In accepting that you were either violated or mistreated by whomever, you will be able to forgive them. Forgiveness is key to your healing and walking in the fullness of God's plan for your life. Write the names of those who have wronged you and go through the process of forgiving them one by one, even those who may have died.

It is time to walk in liberty. Forgiveness hinders you from

walking in total freedom. You may also burn up the paper after you have had this time of healing or self-deliverance. Do not be afraid to write beside their names the offence that they have committed against you.

"Bear with each other and forgive one another if any of you has a grievance against someone. Forgive as the Lord forgave you" (Col. 3:13, NIV).

_____

_____

_____

_____

_____

_____

_____

_____

_____

_____

_____

_____

_____

_____

Day 7, Chapter 8
The Better Part

Use the space provided or a journal to document your answer to the instructions for self-reflection.

Throughout the Scriptures we have seen the power of God at work in the lives of many people, and how He turned their mourning into dancing. Let's take, for example, Joseph who was despised by his brothers, sold into slavery, lied on by Potiphar's wife, imprisoned innocently, yet through all of this he held on to his trust in God.

Joseph couldn't see the plan that God had in store for him, but at the end he experienced the better part when the very gift that caused him to be disliked and rejected by his brothers was the gift that was used to elevate him to the right hand of Pharaoh as his Governor.

Today, God has a better part awaiting you as you surrender your all to Him. God will allow you to walk into what He has already in place waiting for you.

Many times we pray and fast and it seems like nothing is happening, but today my challenge to you is to begin to practice being still and listen to what God is saying to you in this season through the art of silence.

Yes! Be silent for at least three hours and wait in the presence of God.

Step 1. Choose a day where you know you will not be distracted. It may be that you will have to be intentional about this time.

Step 2. Set a time, it could be from 6:00 a.m. to 12:00 noon. That means you begin to condition your mind from the day before and begin to pray about this time in silence before God.

Step 3. Have with you your Bible, your journal, and do not speak at all.

Step 4. Wait in His presence with silence as Mary did. She was quiet at His feet and absorbed every word that came forth from His lips. Allow His Word to speak and listen for the Holy Spirit to speak. At the end of this period of silence, offer up thanks unto the Lord for the time spent and what He has done in you. Thank Him, too, for the opportunity to be still and listen.

"I wait for the Lord, my whole being waits, and in his word I put my hope" (Psalms 130:5, NIV).

GRATEFUL ACKNOWLEDGEMENTS

First, I want to thank my Lord and Savior Jesus Christ, whose love and grace have kept me all these years.

To my husband, Hopeton, you have been a tower of strength to me. You have constantly motivated me to not only dream but to start living the dream. I love you.

To my parents: mother, father, stepmother, and stepfather who played their role in helping me to become the woman I am today. Thank you for giving me the strength and support I needed as I penned this book.

To my sister who believed in me and encouraged me to push forward and be all that I was called to be. To my dearest friends and my prayer partners (a group of women who bear me up in prayers constantly, support me in my lowest moments, and rejoice with me in my victories), I am forever grateful.

Zajavia, Judah and Joshua, I am blessed to call you my children. Thank you for loving me the way you do and being patient with me during my time of writing.

To Kamaaleo, my brother and dearest friend, who

never stopped encouraging me and watering my soul with the word of God and your friendship. You have been a mentor and my personal editor for everything. I am eternally grateful to you.

To Ruth, my publisher, who dared and helped me to step out in obedience to God and share my story with the world, I am grateful.

To all those who took the time to read the manuscript, thank you.

To Dr Felicia Grey, thank you for your excellent foreword.

To Sophia Gabriel and Sherele Robinson, thank you for your endorsements. Sherele, thank you also for your attentiveness in listening whenever I call you.

Last, but not least, to my older prayer mothers who have journeyed with me for so many years, I am grateful for how the Lord has used you all to help in my spiritual formation. I cannot forget the men like my Pastor, John Miller, and the others who invested, not only in my spiritual life, but my personal life. Thank you all, and I am honored to have such a wonderful support system.

ABOUT THE AUTHOR

Georgia Haffenden is a native of the beautiful island of Jamaica, who now resides in Edmonton, Alberta, Canada with her husband and three children. She grew up in the 'garden parish' of St. Ann.

Georgia holds a Bachelor of Social Work degree from the Jamaica Theological Seminary. She served as a Social Worker in the parish of St. Mary, at the Annotto Bay Hospital for over ten years, and later at the Port Maria Hospital's Child and Adolescent Health Clinic. She is also an ordained minister who has been actively involved in sharing the gospel of Jesus Christ in Jamaica, the United States and Canada.

For the past fifteen years, she has committed herself to the call of being a servant in God's

Kingdom, and continues to avail herself to those she has been called to serve. She enjoys preaching and teaching the Word of God. She has mentored and discipled many who have expressed their desire to walk in their purpose, as well as to know more about Christ.

Georgia is a member of the Berean Church of God International in Edmonton, and is presently completing a Master of Divinity at Taylor College and Seminary in Edmonton, Alberta. She has great expectations to further complete a PhD.

Georgia is motivated by this text from Isaiah 6:8, "Then I heard the voice of the Lord saying, "Whom shall I send? And who will go for us?" And I said, "Here am I. Send me!" This is her prayer daily as she humbles herself, and continues to march forward for the sake of the Gospel of Jesus Christ.

REFERENCES

Promundo and UN Women [2017]. "Understanding Masculinities: Results from the Internatio- nal Men and Gender Equality Survey (IMAGES) – Middle East and North Africa."
https://www.unwomen.org/media/headquarters/attachments/sections/library/publications/2017/images-mena-multi-country-report-en.pdf?la=en&vs=3602

UNICEF (2017). "A Familiar Face: Violence in the Lives of Children and Adolescents."
https://www.unicef.org/publications/files/Violence_in_the_lives_of_children_and_adolescents.pdf

United Nations Office on Drugs and Crime (2019). "Global Study on Homicide."
https://www.unodc.org/documents/data-and-analysis/gsh/Booklet1.pdf

World Health Organization (2013). "Global and Regional Estimates of Violence Against Women: Prevalence and Health Effects of Intimate Partner Violence and Non-Partner Sexual Violence."

133

https://apps.who.int/iris/bitstream/handle/106
65/85239/9789241564625_eng.pdf;jsessionid=
A671C2C3D1FD9E5F0D44D5D81352AD14?se
que

Made in the USA
Middletown, DE
29 June 2020